The Anger HABIT™ workbook

Proven Principles to Calm the Stormy Mind

Carl Semmelroth, PhD

SOURCEBOOKS, INC.®
NAPERVILLE, ILLINOIS

W9-CDH-582

Published by Sourcebooks, Inc.
P.O. Box 4410, Naperville, Illinois 60567-4410
(630) 961-3900
FAX: (630) 961-2168
www.sourcebooks.com

Originally published in 2002

ISBN: 1-4022-0335-7

Printed and bound in the United States of America
VP 10 9 8 7 6 5 4 3 2 1

Acknowledgments

Enthusiastic feedback and encouragement from family, friends, and professional colleagues were the author's sustenance that made completion of *The Anger Habit Workbook* possible.

My wife, Sara Semmelroth, seasoned therapist, best friend, and professional colleague, read and commented on each chapter as it was written. Likewise, my daughter, Jean Unroe, seasoned therapist and professional colleague, read and made many helpful comments on the manuscript. My daughter, Melissa, the most courageous person I know, supplied cheerleading and endless unconditional support through thick and thin.

The generous help of professional colleagues with diverse psychological points of view has continued to sharpen the approach to anger problems presented here. Especially helpful have been discussions with Drs. Dale M. Brethower, Donald E. P. Smith, and Hal Weidner.

Finally, my debt to Louise Waller, editor of this book, grows yet larger. A veteran psychology editor for several large publishing houses, she once again took time from her busy retirement to edit another book. Her line-by-line editing, overall suggestions, and supportive comments gently transformed the manuscript into a book.

Contents

Introduction: How to Use This Book

The design of this book is intended to make it useful for individuals or groups working on anger management. Chapters can be used independently and in any order.

If you are a therapist or leader of an anger management group, you can easily design your own curriculum using chapters that fit the needs of those you are helping. If you are an individual using the book on your own, you can pick and choose chapters with topics that suit you. You do need to read lesson 1 because it gives an overview of how to approach anger problems. Lessons contain specific exercises with examples of how to carry them out.

We strongly suggest that you keep a private notebook or journal while working through the book. At the end of most lessons are examples of how to record successes in making "real life" changes. These successes can be recorded in your own notebook. It is well and good to gain insight and understanding of anger problems, but recording "real life" successes will help you to generate life changes that make all the difference.

Lesson 1:
A Third Way to Manage Anger

Ralph, usually a quiet and well-mannered high school student, suddenly went into a rage one day after school. Two fellow students passed by him after school and one of them turned and said, "How's girl-boy today? Is she headed home to Mommy?" After they passed, Ralph picked up a two-by-four from a construction site they were near. He ran up behind the two students striking one over the head, crushing the back of his skull.

Sally was a very angry woman. Her childhood had been unhappy, and she was in a marriage that increasingly consisted of little more than angry arguments with her husband. She spent two years in therapy trying to learn to communicate her anger appropriately to her husband. She also worked at confronting her parents with her anger at them for neglecting her feelings when she was a child. Sally's life didn't seem to be getting any better.

It is common wisdom that people should not hold back their anger, like Ralph had always done, because it will damage them.

Smothering anger not only causes unhappiness and stress, it also makes it more likely that there will be a serious destructive outbreak of anger sometime in the future.

It seems natural that in order to keep from smothering anger, you need to learn to express it, albeit in nondestructive ways. This way of approaching anger concentrates on learning where your anger comes from, communicating your anger, and finally confronting those who caused you to be angry, as Sally tried to do.

This book teaches a third alternative to suppressing or expressing anger; namely, learning to solve problems in ways that don't involve anger.

The first alternative, smothering anger like Ralph did, is a bad idea. The reason that smothering anger is dangerous is found in the nature of anger itself. The feeling of anger is your awareness of your preparation to attack someone to punish or control them. The opposite of preparing to attack is to prepare to run away. So smothering anger feels like a defeat. It feels as if you have been wronged and are a victim; but instead of asserting your "rights," you have turned tail and let the person who has wronged you get away with it.

When you handle your anger in this way, you become a powder keg with a ready-to-go fuse. There will come a time when, accidentally or otherwise, something or someone will light that fuse through an act that you see as so outrageously unfair that you will no longer smother your response. Even a small event, when mixed with your thoughts of, "I've had enough," can set off a righteous and destructive explosion. Then you will give yourself permission to do really awful and destructive things in the name of righteousness.

The second alternative is to learn to express anger in some nondestructive way. Confronting and communicating, as Sally tried to do, are favorite ways. If you were a hydraulic machine, and anger was a hydraulic liquid that built up pressure when it had no place to go, then, yes, you would need to find some way to "let off" the pressure. But anger is not like pressure in a steam engine or hydraulic liquid in a hose. Anger is a set of behaviors. And, unfortunately, many of those behaviors are habits.

Expressing anger, constructively or otherwise, is not the only alternative to smothering it.

A third alternative is to examine anger as a behavior, a behavior that has as its goal the solution to a problem. This provides you with something to do other than acting on your anger. It also provides you with an alternative to feeling defeated and unjustly treated. It identifies the problem that your anger was directed at. Solving that problem without anger makes all the difference.

Feeling angry means that you, through habit, have chosen a solution to a problem that has arisen. It means that you have chosen attack as your problem-solving tool. Having a problem with your anger means that you use attack as the tool to solve many problems in your life.

Choosing other ways to solve problems does not require smothering anger or expressing anger. It just means you no longer automatically reach for that one tool, attack, to solve your problems.

Expressing anger in any way—harmful or harmless—does not solve the real problem of anger. It is more likely to keep your anger present than it is to dispel it. Consider, does laughing reduce your good disposition, or does it keep it around? Does acting on fear make you a less fearful person or does it make it more likely that you will be fearful in the future?

These are feelings that go with certain behaviors, just as anger is a feeling that goes with certain behaviors. Why is it then that expressing anger is expected to reduce it? Anger can result in a set of behaviors when certain problems are experienced. Using these behaviors makes it more likely that they will continue to be used, not less likely—thus, the anger habit.

This book teaches you the third way to deal with anger. It guides you through the learning of new habits for the solution of problems that you commonly "solve" with anger. Learning alternatives to anger instead of smothering it or expressing it reduces its presence in your life.

Your reward for working to reduce anger is much greater than just reducing "blowups" or even stopping the destructive and irrational behaviors that accompany anger. These are worthy, important, and satisfying goals of anger management. But this book guides you toward much more than the management or control of your anger.

Anger produces a stormy mind as well as a stormy life. It entangles you in struggles with others. It reduces your sense of freedom. It makes communication difficult, if not impossible, and without communication, relationships wither on the vine. Anger impairs your intelligence.

It leads you into a life dominated by a perpetual desire to control even more than you actually control, and to accumulate the power to do so. And it preoccupies you with the problem of keeping what you control now under your control forever.

The rewards for giving up the anger habit are: a calm mind, a sense of freedom, better communication with others, a more refined intelligence, more satisfying relationships, release from the quest for power, and the comfort and vitality that come with a life that encourages others, rather than a life bent on controlling them.

It is important for you to complete the exercises contained in each lesson in order to achieve these goals. Just understanding your anger habit will not change it. It takes practice to develop a new attitude, an attitude of problem-solving in place of controlling and attacking.

Examples of "answers" are included with every exercise as guides for your written responses. Sometimes it helps to get started by copying one of the examples and letting it become your own as you write.

It will also be helpful for you to find a friend, counselor, or family member with whom you can discuss issues that arise as you work through the lessons. If you are using the book in an anger management class or group, the group will supply the opportunity to discuss issues as they occur.

Finally, as you work through the lessons in this workbook, you will find advice on how to keep a record of your successes at changing the way you deal with problems. Examples are provided, but you will need a diary or private notebook to keep a record of your successful progress. It is important to recognize and record your successes. They will help you sustain your efforts and serve as models for you to continue solving problems without anger in the future.

A calm mind will strengthen you. It will give you peace. It will reward your efforts to achieve it.

Lesson 2:
How to Cool Your Anger Down

Before we get to the problem of reducing how often you get angry, you must learn how to cool down from anger when it seems to have control of you. This is your most difficult lesson for a very good reason. When you are angry, you aren't very smart. One reason anger causes so much destruction and unhappiness is:

• As your anger goes up, your IQ goes down.

It is difficult for you to stop being angry after your anger takes hold because you aren't very smart when you're angry. So, all the things that you tell yourself to do about your anger when you are calm are tuned out when you are angry. Think how hard it is to step in and calm friends when they get angry. You try to tell them that the anger isn't worth it, that they are blowing things out of proportion, that they aren't being reasonable.

How much good does all this solid advice do? Usually not much. And that's just the point:

- When we are angry, we are unreasonable.

Other people are unreasonable when they're angry, and so are you. Other people don't listen to good advice when they're angry, and you don't either. When we are angry and unreasonable and won't follow good advice, we sometimes do some pretty dumb things. Angry people are even apt to put themselves and their loved ones in danger. Other people drive dangerously when they are angry. You may also drive dangerously when you are angry.

Other people attack their children physically and verbally when they are angry. You are apt to endanger your loved ones when you are angry. And that is because:

- When we are angry, we do dangerous things.

Add it up. When you are angry…

- Your IQ goes down.
- You are unreasonable.
- You are likely to endanger yourself and/or those you love.

Exercise 2-A: What You Are Like When You Are Angry

Recall two times you have been angry and did something not very smart as a result. Write down what you did and why it wasn't too bright. These two examples will help you get the idea.

Example 1: I got angry with a driver that cut me off. I sped up (over the speed limit) and cut him off. It was stupid because he could have easily run into me and caused a fatal accident, and my children were in the car.

Example 2: My husband embarrassed me when we were out with friends and I didn't speak to him for two days. It wasn't a very good idea because I was more miserable for the two days than he was.

Write our your own examples for Exercise 2-A.

Your example 1:

_____

_____

_____

_____

_____

Your example 2:

_____

_____

_____

_____

_____

Because you aren't as smart and reasonable when you are angry as you are when you are calm, you need to have some very simple things to say to yourself when you are angry. You will not listen to yourself and calm down if you say things that are too complicated or sophisticated.

For example, if you try to tell yourself that you are blowing things out of proportion and the person you are angry at is really a friend, you are not likely to calm down with these overly complicated and abstract ideas. Most of us cannot listen to ourselves when we get heated up in anger. We can say the words to ourselves: "I'm blowing this all out of proportion." But it sure doesn't feel like that at the time. So we aren't often able to really make a difference in our anger by trying to calm ourselves down that way. A simple, straightforward way to approach yourself when you are angry is to remind yourself that you are not very bright when you are angry. Learn to say to yourself:

- I'm angry, so I may do something stupid.
- I don't want to turn my life over to someone who is mentally impaired, namely me.
- A dummy is deciding anything I do or say right now.

If you have a problem and want advice on what to do or say in some situation, who is it you choose to guide you? Do you seek out the most stupid person you know and do what they say? Of course not. You look for someone who is bright and reasonable to help you decide what to do. If that person isn't immediately available, aren't you willing to wait at least fifteen minutes for them to appear?

Well, when you are angry, if you wait fifteen minutes, someone will appear who is bright and reasonable and will give you advice about what to do. That person is you. An intelligent and reasonable you will be along in a little while to make your decisions. Telling yourself you are not very bright sounds negative. But in this case, it's kind of a sneaky compliment. You are recognizing that most of the time you live your life intelligently and solve your problems reasonably. This is a compliment. You will not feel put down nor will you feel that you are smothering your anger. The problem that led to anger will still be there for an intelligent you to consider later.

It is just that you aren't going to do or say anything to solve that problem while you are in a mentally impaired state.

Exercise 2-B:
Learning That Waiting Makes You Smarter

Think of two situations when you were angry and later discovered that the problem you were angry about could be solved in a reasonable way. Write down what you did when you were angry, what the problems turned out to be, and how you actually solved the problems. These two examples will help you see what to do.

Example 1: I asked my daughter to baby-sit her younger sister while I went to the store. She said she was too busy. I lost it and lit into her. Later I realized that she had a test the next day, and I asked my neighbor to look after Sally for a few minutes while I went to the store.

Example 2: I couldn't get the lawn mower started and got really mad. It was nearly new, and I wanted to go storming over to the dealer and tell him what a piece of junk he had sold me. I thought I'd better try to start the Weed Eater first. It occurred to me that I hadn't checked to see if the mower deck was raised. I checked and it wasn't. I raised it and the mower started right up.

Your example 1:

_____

_____

_____

_____

_____

Your example 2:

_____
_____
_____
_____
_____

Learning to take time out until your intelligence returns requires a lot of practice. Anger doesn't completely subside over fifteen or twenty minutes if you continue to feed the flames with angry thoughts. Thoughts of injustice or thoughts of how you were wronged in some way most often feed anger.

Some common thoughts that fuel anger and keep it burning even while time passes are:

- I always have to do all the work.
- He/she never learns.
- This is always what I get.
- He/she never gives a crap.

The one best sign to you that indicates you are fueling your anger is when you are thinking "always" or "never" about something.

So remember:
Thinking "always" or "never" always makes things worse and never solves anything.

When someone keeps thinking thoughts like these, that person will stay dumb and angry, even if they don't act on the anger. The time needed to become intelligent again must be filled with something other than thoughts that fuel the anger.

Exercise 2-C:
Identifying Your "Favorite" Anger Fuel

Think of at least two situations or people that make you angry. That is, when you think about them now, you can feel anger coming back. What thoughts do you have that you could use to keep yourself angry with them if you wanted to stay angry? Write down some of the thoughts and how they amount to some wrong that you feel has been done to you. These two examples will guide you.

Example 1: My husband *never* listens. He *always* stares off into space while I'm talking. He didn't bring home what I asked him to this morning. I *always* listen to him, so he should listen to me.

Example 2: The children *always* make a mess. They get food out of the refrigerator and *always* leave stuff all over the counters. John *always* leaves wrenches all over the floor in the garage from working on his bike, and I'm *never* able to drive in when I get home. The children should listen to me when I tell them to stop doing something.

Your example 1:

_____

_____

_____

_____

_____

_____

Your example 2:

_____

_____

_____

_____

_____

_____

Thoughts like these are what fuel your anger and maintain it even when you are not expressing it. They help to keep your intelligence low and prevent you from solving your problems in a reasonable way that doesn't hurt your interests or loved ones. Don't think that you must give up the idea of being justly treated and just let everything go on as it is now in order to manage your anger. Quite the contrary, letting go of the thought of having been unjustly treated allows you to calm down so that you can solve whatever problem there is with your head.

Deciding what to do about unruly children, a boss who makes unfair assignments, a reckless driver, a spouse that does unkind things, or any other problem you may encounter is best carried out when you are calm. In order to become calm, you:

- Tell yourself that you are angry, and if you act or talk while you are angry you will probably do or say something stupid.
- Tell yourself that when you are calm you can identify and solve the problem.
- Tell yourself to divert your thinking from the "fuel for anger thoughts" to something else until the feeling of anger goes away.

Now that you know what to do about getting your IQ back to where it should be, you need to practice doing it. It will be extremely helpful to keep a record of your successes for a while.

Record your successes in a private notebook or diary. Set up a practice record for Lesson 2 in your private notebook using the two examples given below as a model. Leave space for at least five examples.

Practice Record For Lesson 2

Example 1: Date: 9/01

Incident: I was trying to find some papers I needed and looked everywhere. I was thinking my wife had moved them and that she always does that and I was really getting frustrated and worked up.

What I did: For once, instead of accusing my wife and starting a fight, I told myself I was angry, and while I'm feeling this way I am probably going to do something pretty dumb. I tried to stop thinking "always" and "never" thoughts about my wife by going out and mowing the lawn and thinking about the things I want to do with the lawn.

Success: When I came back into the house, it occurred to me that the papers I was looking for might be in my briefcase. That's where they were.

Example 2: Date: 9/7

Incident: I was driving to work and in a hurry. Traffic was all backed up, as it always is, and I started to get really tense and angry.

What I did: I was trying to find an opening in another lane to force myself in when it occurred to me that I was angry and was probably going to do something stupid. I turned the radio to some music rather than the upsetting news stories I usually listen to, and relaxed my body and looked around at all the cars and tense-looking people.

Success: I started thinking of how I could get some tapes from the library of books that I had always wanted to read and keep them in the car so I'd have something interesting to do when driving to work. I was thinking about that off and on all day and went to the library after work.

Lesson 3:
Learning to Own the Cause of Your Anger

Where does your anger come from? It feels as if other people are the cause of your anger. But is that true? "They make me so angry!" is something you probably have said more than once. Is it really true that you make other people angry and they make you angry? If it is true that we make each other angry, then we have control of other people's anger and they have control of our anger. So, according to this way of thinking, husbands and wives have control of each other's anger; children have control of their parents' anger; and victims have control of their victimizers' anger. That would mean that anger management classes would need to be about how you keep others from getting angry and hurting you. But that's ridiculous.

Anger is a way we have of trying to control something or someone. It is a tool we possess from the time we are born.

The anger tool is designed to cause something unpleasant to happen to someone. Babies cry and howl, a very unpleasant and unwelcome sound for parents and others. Adults yell and threaten, a very unpleasant experience for loved ones and friends. Spouses pout and freeze up, a very unpleasant experience for their partners. And robbers point guns at their victims—unpleasant and frightening.

It requires a perverse inverting of responsibility to think of victims as being in control of the attacks and threats that others aim at them.

So, despite how it might feel to you:
You are responsible for your anger.

Your feeling of anger is just your awareness that you are getting ready to attack someone. It is similar to your feeling of sexual arousal. When you are sexually aroused, it just means that your body is getting ready to have sex. Angry feelings are anger arousal. They just mean that you are getting ready to attack. These are *your feelings* and they signal *your preparation to attack*.

Sexual feelings don't cause you to have sex, nor do they mean you must have sex, nor are they a reason to have sex. Similarly,

- Angry feelings don't cause you to attack.
- Angry feelings don't mean you must attack.
- Angry feelings aren't a reason to attack.

And as with sex, how you perceive what's going on makes a big difference. Your arousal to angry feelings diminishes quickly if the way you see the situation changes. For example, if someone hits you on the shoulder from behind, and upon turning to look, you see an old friend smiling at you, the hit is unlikely to "cause" you to be angry.

Exercise 3-A:
Seeing Anger as Your Own

Think of something that almost always makes you angry. Get into it. Get your anger going by just thinking of it. Write down a short description of what you are thinking. Then notice how your body feels when you are thinking this way and write it down. Is there anything about how you are feeling that requires you to attack, or even gives you a reason to attack? Notice how different the feeling of your anger is from the thoughts you are having that got you going. Here's an example:

Example of an anger-producing thought: I'm thinking of a time when I was a child outside of the school building during recess. This kid came up to me and started saying things about my older sister, like she was a whore, and everybody has had her.

My feeling: My body is tense. I feel an unpleasant feeling around my eyes. My shoulders are up a little. As I imagine hitting, I can feel my right hand and arm starting to make a fist.

Is there anything about the feeling that makes you have to attack? These are just body feelings when I separate them from my thoughts about the playground situation. And they are not very pleasant feelings.

Your example of an anger-producing thought:

_____

_____

_____

_____

Your feeling:

_____

_____

_____

_____

Is there anything about the feeling that makes you have to attack?

_____

_____

_____

_____

So, if others don't cause your anger and your feelings don't cause your attacks, what is responsible for your angry feelings, your angry words, and your angry deeds?

The answer is:
Anger is your attempt to solve a problem by seizing control.

It is easier to see that anger is an attempt to control other people when we look at anger in others than it is to see it in us. You have seen children have temper tantrums and can easily identify them as attempts of these children (or adults) to get their way. You know what it feels like when someone is angry with you. You know the feeling you have when your behavior is not what others want it to be.

In other words:
You know what it feels like to have others attempt to control you through their anger.

You may not always know what others want when they are angry with you, but you know darn well you did something "wrong" in their eyes. And you know that they are making your behavior their business. Consider then, when you get angry, what are *you* doing?

What you are doing is trying to make other people's behavior *your* business.

Exercise 3-B:
What Do Others Who Are Angry With You Want?

Try to remember three different times someone has been angry with you. Write these down along with what you think the person wanted you to do. The two examples will help you get the idea.

Example 1: I stopped at a light and didn't start up right away when the light turned green. The car behind me stood on his horn even after I had started moving. He wanted me to not inconvenience him by delaying his trip by a couple seconds.

Example 2: My husband yelled at me when I came home with a new dress. He wants to control how I spend my money.

Your example 1:

_____

_____

_____

_____

Your example 2:

_____

_____

_____

_____

Your example 3:

_____

_____

_____

_____

_____

These are examples of how others try to control your behavior by showing they are willing to attack you verbally or even physically. Now you need to see how your anger is your own doing and how you use it to try to get what you want.

Exercise 3-C: What Do You Want When You Are Angry?

Think of three times you have been angry. Write them down, along with a description of the person you were trying to control and what behavior of theirs you were trying to take charge of.

These two examples will help you get started:

Example 1: My boss gave someone else the available overtime work. This is the second time in a month he's done this. I was really angry, but I didn't say anything. I guess I was prepared to attack him to make him assign me more overtime.

Example 2: The children were even more noisy than usual while I was trying to talk on the phone. I yelled at them and sent them to their rooms. I was trying to make them be quiet by attacking them verbally and controlling where they spent the next ten minutes.

Your example 1:

_____

_____

_____

_____

Your example 2:

_____

_____

_____

_____

Your example 3:

_____

_____

_____

_____

Anger isn't a force that makes you act in angry ways. It is something you do to solve a problem. If you have an anger problem, it is because you use the tool of anger to solve those problems. You are like a mechanic with only one tool—perhaps a hammer. Every new problem immediately becomes a nail and the hammer gets used again. Many people use anger as their favorite tool for solving problems. They have a habit of using anger. They have the anger habit.

Getting rid of the anger habit takes a lot of practice, but there are rewards along the way.

You are probably still working on getting your IQ back up when you get angry—the exercise at the end of lesson 2. The more often you wait until you achieve perspective and approach a problem intelligently, the better you will feel. The more adult you will feel. The more in control you will feel. So keep it up.

This lesson asks you to own your anger. That really goes against the grain. It is even part of our language to speak of situations and people that "make us angry." At first you might feel like you are taking all the blame when you view anger as a tool you use, rather than something that others cause you to feel. Working at owning your anger has its rewards. The big prize you will win is to find that others can't control you if you don't try to control them.

If you haven't yet set up a private notebook or diary for recording your successful achievements in overcoming your anger, please try it. Set up a practice record for lesson 3 in your private notebook using the two examples given below as a model. Leave space for at least five examples situations that "made you angry" but you were able to see that your anger was your attempt to change something.

Practice Record For Lesson Three

Example 1: Date: 10/1
Situation that "made me angry": My significant other promised to call me and didn't.
What I wanted: After a while I realized that my anger was not something he made me have. I was getting ready to make his life miserable to punish him so he wouldn't do that again.

Example 2: Date: 10/2
Situation that "made me angry": My mother called and kept asking and asking all about what I was doing like she always does.
What I wanted: After thinking about it, I realized that I don't really have to tell her anything other than what I wish. My anger was me trying to hurt her so she wouldn't talk to me this way.

Lesson 4:
Do You Really Want Control?

Anger is about control. We "get" angry when things don't go the way we expect or want them to go. We either make things unpleasant for others by attacking them so that things will change, or, if we don't actually attack them, we feel ourselves getting ready to attack. The feeling that goes with our preparation for attack is the feeling of anger.

The anger or the attack is about trying to control things so that they will change. But what does it mean to control things? Is control something you really want a lot of? You think you do, but do you? If you have lots of control it means you will need to do a lot of work. Here's why.

In order to control people, you must at all times make sure they do not have desires and opportunities to behave in ways other than those *you* wish them to have. Control of others isn't something you can acquire like a new car or a house. Once you get most things, you have them and can keep them. Control over others isn't like that. Control is something that you must constantly work at. Like a taxi meter, it keeps on ticking; it keeps on costing you as long as you want to keep it. Think of what it takes to control you. Are you a sheep that just goes along with the crowd?

Even if you are a sheep, have you ever noticed how much work sheepdogs must do to control their flocks? They must always be alert and ready to head off any break with herd conformity. But you aren't a sheep, and, like most of us, you are sensitive to others' attempts to control your behavior.

Think of how much work it would take for other people to control you when you don't want them to be in control. What would they need to do to really be in control of your behavior? They would need to watch you at all times and be sure that you never chose to do anything that they didn't approve of. That would require them to be responsible for the consequences of your behavior. If you choose the wrong word in conversation, they will have to know it and have some mechanism for "feeding" you information that will "correct" you. If you go to the bathroom at the wrong time, they will have to know it and have some mechanism for stopping you. Control over you by others would require:
1. Constant monitoring of your behavior; and/or
2. Manipulation of all the consequences of your behavior.

One way to think about the control of other people is that it requires all the information that they possess plus the power to control that information. It requires that you become "Big Brother."

Exercise 4-A:
How People Try To Control You

Think of three situations where you resented other people's attempts to control you. Describe the situations, the method used to attempt control, and the use of information in that attempt. The two examples will help get you started.

Example 1: My boss wanted me to take on extra work that really isn't part of my job.

Method of control: The deal was, either do it or make the boss unhappy. I didn't want to, but I did it.

Use of information in attempt to control: Well, the boss always checks up on what I'm doing, so he's in a position to know whether I do what he asked. He also let me know that I wouldn't get treated very well if I didn't comply. And he's in a position to make that real information, that is, he can make that happen.

Example 2: My husband wanted to buy a new car. I didn't think it was a very good idea.

Method of control: He kept telling me how much our current car would cost us in repairs. When I argued with him, he got really sullen. After a couple weeks of his not talking very much and the house being like a funeral parlor, I gave up.

Use of information in attempt to control: My husband tried feeding me a line about how it would be financially best if we had a new car. When that didn't wash, he did every thing he could to communicate that I was going to be miserable until he got his way.

Your example 1:

_____

_____

_____

_____

Method of control:

_____

_____

_____

_____

Use of information in attempt to control:

_____

_____

_____

_____

Your example 2:

_____

_____

_____

_____

Method of control:

_____

_____

_____

_____

Use of information in attempt to control:

_____

_____

_____

_____

Your example 3:

_____

_____

_____

_____

Method of control:

_____

_____

_____

_____

Use of information in attempt to control:

_____

_____

_____

_____

Others clearly need to go to great lengths to control you and probably aren't always successful. Control uses up a great amount of resources. It literally requires enough power to control what happens to people no matter how they try to escape from your control. Think of the resources required to confine people in prisons, and they don't actually control much of prisoners' behavior. Think of how much power an intrusive government needs and the resources it requires in order to control its citizens.

Do you really want to be in the control business? Your anger says you do. It is the sign that you are acting as if you want to control a lot of things around you. Others avoid your control attempts, just as you avoid control attempts by them. And that leads to even more anger and more time and resources devoted to the struggle by everyone involved.

A useful rule for persons, organizations, businesses, and government is:

Leave everything as voluntary as you possibly can.

This rule dramatically reduces the amount of energy and resources needed to keep a person, organization, business, or government healthy and happy.

Unfortunately, you are probably running your life with the opposite rule:

Make everything that is voluntary, as involuntary as you can.

Many businesses and the supervisors they employ do this and eventually ruin a good business. Perhaps you have worked somewhere where month after month, year after year, things you did on your job voluntarily were made requirements of the job.

Well, maybe you do that same thing in your relationships and your life. Ask yourself:

- Do you require things of your spouse that you didn't in the beginning?
- Do you require things of family members that you didn't in the beginning?
- Do you require drivers on the road to drive perfectly?
- Do you require people to think about you in certain ways that you didn't when you were younger?

- Do you require physical possessions that you only wished for or enjoyed before?
- Do you require that your future go just a certain way, when earlier in your life you were comfortable with an uncertain future?

The more you attempt to control the people and things around you, the more burdensome your life becomes and the angrier you are. Think carefully about some relationship you have that isn't much fun anymore. Ask yourself, what have I done over the years to try to control this person's behavior? What has it cost me? Do I really want to continue trying to control this person?

Exercise 4-B: Recognizing the Cost of Control

There are three areas in which you most likely are trying to exert control, and therefore that contribute to some of your anger—a relationship, your future, and the way others view you. Pick a relationship, something about the future, and something about the way others view you and describe each one. Try to estimate how much effort control of each costs you. Consider whether it is really worth it to you. There are examples for each of these three areas of control to guide you.

A relationship that you try to control

Example 1: My wife doesn't have sex with me very often. I get really angry about it sometimes. I guess this anger must be me trying to control her. Sometimes I blow up at her and call her frigid. Sometimes I accuse her of having an affair.

What my control attempt costs: This is easy. Things are really miserable for days at a time after our fights about sex. Sometimes she will consent to have sex, and then cries or is really cold afterward. I can't even touch her or hug her; or she pulls away and accuses me of just wanting her to service me. I hurt inside a lot and am angry a lot.

Is it worth it? I'd have to say absolutely not. I can't force her into sex by threatening and blowing up without her just doing it to get it over with. I don't want that. I must let go of my attempts to control her—leave her alone about it. If she doesn't do it voluntarily, then it is no good. Maybe we can talk about it after I lay off her for a while.

Your example 1:

_____

_____

_____

_____

_____

What my control attempt costs:

_____

_____

_____

_____

_____

Is it worth it?

_____

_____

_____

_____

_____

Future that you try to control

Example 2: Future that I'm trying to control: I want my children to be very good students and go to college and be successful. I'm always after them to take school more seriously. I get angry with them about any grade less than an A, and there are lots of lower grades showing up. I try to make them do their homework, but I can't always be there. So I have to rely on what they tell me. Later, when they get their grades, I find out they lied and I ground them. But it doesn't seem to do any good.

What my control attempt costs: It seems as if the more I get angry with the kids, the worse they do and the less honest they are with me. Susie doesn't even act as if she wants to be around me any more. That hurts. I can't talk to the kids about their futures without them rolling their eyes and taking off at the first opportunity. I could go to half-time at my job and always pick them up from school and stand over them. But that seems like too much.

Is it worth it? Well, what I'm doing isn't worth it. The children are just learning to hate school and me. And I'm scared for them and angry a lot. Maybe I need to lay off all the talk and anger and just do what I can do. I can always see that they do some homework. If they say their teachers didn't give them any, I can give them some. At least I can see how they are doing in their subjects; and maybe we can talk about things if I stop attacking them and just stand my ground and stay with them while they study. I can do that and not get angry. Their future is going to have to be up to them.

Your example 2:

_____

_____

_____

_____

_____

What my control attempt costs:

_____

_____

_____

_____

_____

Is it worth it?

_____

_____

_____

_____

_____

Another's view of me that I try to control

Example 3: What I'm trying to control about the way others view me: Well, I want my family and others to view me as strong, able to solve problems, and always confidant. A lot of the time I'm not very confident, but I find myself coming across as sure of myself. If the kids or my wife or people at work challenge me, I verbally attack them. I can see that this is just my way of trying to make them think I'm always right.

What my control attempt costs: I really have to be on guard for when people don't think of me as knowing everything and always having the answer. I need to defend positions that I don't even believe in. This makes me feel isolated. A lot of times I can feel that people think I'm a. fool. My children, who used to ask me everything, can hardly stand hearing what I have to say now. My wife doesn't even argue anymore. She just says, "You know everything."

Is it worth it? No way. Now I can see that my anger at the children and my wife is my attempt to control the way they view me. I don't really have to appear so confident and strong and all-knowing to others. They will think what they think. Maybe I'll try being a little more mysterious. That wouldn't be hard for me to do. I never know half the time what to think about what's going on anyway.

Your example 3:

_____

_____

_____

_____

_____

What my control attempt costs me:

_____

_____

_____

_____

_____

Is it worth it?

_____

_____

_____

_____

_____

It is very helpful to identify control attempts as the source of your anger. Maybe you wish to continue to try to control others in certain situations. But when you see how often you are angry as a result, you will soon get an idea of how much of a load this kind of control has accumulated over the years. You might want to drop some of that load. For example, thinking angry thoughts and rant-ing and raving—at the TV or your favorite sports team or the gov-ernment or the news—are not ever going to control these people and events that are clearly beyond your control. Do you want to go on acting as if Dan Rather is your child and will shape up if you threaten him?

Chances are you have taken on the burden of controlling a good part of the world. Why would you want to keep that burden? Especially since, judging from the state of the world, you're obvi-ously doing such a lousy job of it.

Lesson 5:
Righteous Anger

Anger is about control, but it isn't only about control. Once we get beyond our rather barbaric young childhood, we learn that anger is also about justice. We get angry when we feel we have a fair complaint. People argue heatedly to determine who took advantage of or hurt the other one first or most. Most marital arguments are about who has been victimized the most and therefore has the "right" to be angry.

- Young children learn to say:
  "Yes, I hit him, but he teased me."

- Parents who shake their babies, injuring and sometimes killing them, say:
  "Yes, but the baby's screaming was driving me crazy."

- Husbands who assault their wives say:
  "Yes, but she wouldn't leave me alone."

- And spouses who say and do nasty things to each other say:
  "Yes, but that's nothing compared to what you do."

We use anger to try to get what we want, yes. But usually we only give ourselves permission to use the tool of anger when we are able to see ourselves as victims. You need to understand two things about your anger when it feels justified:

1. Even if you are the victim of another person's unjust behavior, your anger is just a tool you are using to change that. It may not be the best tool.
2. Viewing yourself as a victim may be a habit you have. You may not be the victim you think you are.

First, let's look at number one. Even when you are clearly "in the right," angry attacks are hardly ever your best choice for trying to get justice. There are exceptions. Someone comes running through the yard while you're sitting on the porch and swoops up your two-year-old. Of course you're going to turn immediately into a dangerous machine, perhaps capable of running down and effectively assaulting the kidnapper. But this kind of situation is very rare in most of our lives.

More often you feel "in the right" when someone breaks an agreement with you, or you think they did. Your husband doesn't come home when he said he would. Your friend turns out to have gossiped about you behind your back. Your wife has an affair.

When people break agreements or contracts, we have a right to enforce them.

This does indeed mean we have a right to make their behavior our business. But our anger implies we are getting ready to assault them. That is hardly ever the best way to enforce contracts or agreements.

Exercise 5-A:
Choosing the Right Tool to Enforce Agreements

Think of three incidents when you have gotten angry because you are pretty sure you were "in the right." What was the actual or assumed agreement that was violated by the other party? Assume that because these were situations where you got angry, anger was the first tool you used to enforce the agreement. Think of and describe a better tool you could have used.

These two examples will help guide you.

Example 1: My wife ran up her credit card bills and we had a talk concerning what to do about it. She said she thought she could pay the card off in three months. A month later I saw her statement and she had charged more to the card. I got angry.

The agreement that was violated: My wife had promised she was going to pay off the card, not charge more to it. She broke the promise.

A better tool than anger: I don't think she realizes how important it is to me that she keeps her word to me. It's her card, but if she makes a promise about it she needs to keep that promise. Maybe if we talked again it would help. Maybe I should go with her to a counselor as she's been asking me to do.

Example 2: My so-called friend Amanda was making eyes at my boyfriend at a party. She got him off in a corner where they talked quietly for a while. He looked very uncomfortable, but she was going on with her sweet smile and throwing her big bust up at him.

The agreement that was violated: I guess friendship is a kind of agreement that you won't intentionally hurt your friends or take something they value away from them. Amanda said she was my friend. She violated the promise that goes with being a friend.

A better tool than anger: When I got angry with her, Amanda just got all offended and said I didn't trust her. She tried to turn the tables and make me out to be the one who didn't live up to being a friend. I would have been better off just telling her I don't trust her anymore and then stop calling her. After all, that's the truth. There's no point in trying to change her. At least that's not my job.

Your example 1:

_____

_____

_____

_____

The agreement that was violated:

_____

_____

_____

_____

A better tool than anger:

_____

_____

_____

_____

Your example 2:

_____

_____

_____

_____

The agreement that was violated:

_____

_____

_____

_____

A better tool than anger:

_____

_____

_____

_____

Your example 3:

_____

_____

_____

_____

The agreement that was violated:

_____

_____

_____

_____

A better tool than anger:

_____

_____

_____

_____

Private justice among people is hardly ever best served with anger. Actually, when your anger is most righteous is when you are likely to do the most destructive, inhumane, and irrational things.

When you act on righteous anger, you become the victimizer.

Mahatma Gandhi in South Africa and India, as well as Martin Luther King Jr. in America, guided millions of people away from a violent expression of their righteous anger and won the day without becoming victimizers like their oppressors.

If millions can do it, you too can find ways to redress injustices without making yourself into someone just like your adversary. Remember: Even if you are the victim of another person's unjust behavior, your anger is just a tool you are using to change that. It may not be the best tool.

The second thing about righteous anger already mentioned is: Viewing yourself as a victim may be your habit. You may not be the victim you think you are. You are familiar with "poor me" people. "Poor me" is when we read disappointments, minor setbacks, and just not getting what we want as injustices. We are somehow owed something more desirable than what we get.

Crying "poor me" is a way of demanding from others that they make sure we get what we want because we are owed it. We take for granted that we have a right not to suffer, not to have difficulties, and not to be disappointed. Our response to trouble is to assert our right not to have trouble at all. It is as if our trouble resulted from a broken contract. The assertion of our rights is in the form of anger (getting ready to attack someone to make them make it right) and whining.

Whining is a form of anger that is designed to take advantage of other people's goodwill. We make their goodwill into their duty to help us.

The way to play the victim is:

1. I'm suffering.
2. It's an injustice that I'm suffering.
3. It's the duty of good people to take care of suffering people.
4. It's your duty to take care of me.

And if others don't do their "duty," I am righteously angry. I attack them to make them pay for not giving me what they owe to me, what I'm entitled to.

Chances are good that if you have a problem with anger, you also have a problem with mistaking yourself for a victim. You go seamlessly from not getting what you want or expect to blaming and attacking others or whining and then attacking others when they don't respond to your distress signals. This behavior would make some sense if you had a deal with the rest of the world that said they owed you happiness. Do you have such a deal? Of course not.

Exercise 5-B:
Recognizing Phony Feelings of Injustice

You sometimes feel as if the world has dealt you an injustice. Because it feels like an injustice, you respond with anger. Your anger is your way of demanding that the injustice be fixed. But it isn't always a real injustice. A good place to look for phony feelings of injustice is in your childhood.

Many people carry childhood memories that they interpret as instances of having been treated badly. Unless you were traumatized or beaten or starved as a child, the chances are that you're just whining without reason. This is parent-bashing and it leads to a life-long tendency to feel that every discomfort in life results from someone else's failure to properly take care of you. It is always the government or the lousy landlord or the money-grubbers or the phone company or some other "parent-like" entity, such as your spouse, that causes your problems. Even if the authority didn't cause them, you think that authority owes it to you to fix your problems.

And when they don't, you get angry.

Look for three things you regularly complain about. Look for complaints you make about your parents, a company, some part of government, or someone you treat as somehow being responsible for your happiness. Describe each complaint. Ask yourself, "Do they, or did they, really owe me?" Then try to write down how you might feel if you were able to stop feeling unjustly treated. Use these two examples to get yourself going.

Example 1: Nothing I ever did when I was growing up was good enough. If I got a B in math, it was supposed to be an A. One time I brought home a science project that I had gotten an A on and my dad looked at it and said I should have done it differently. I could never do enough to please him.

Did they really owe me? Well, I've always thought they were lousy parents. Parents owe their children good care. I guess I got pretty good care. Maybe more than pretty good. I guess I just felt so bad for myself back then because I wanted more praise from my parents. I guess they didn't really owe me praise. But it would have made me feel good.

How might I feel if I stopped feeling unjustly treated? For one thing I think I would stop being angry with my parents. I guess that would feel really good. Somehow I think I'd also feel stronger, more like I didn't need to whine, like I'm more in charge of me. Maybe more like an adult!

Example 2: The cable company shut off our cable when I was a little late with the payment. I called them and told them my mother was sick and I had been away a lot and just got behind on the bills. She died two weeks ago, so I'm trying to catch up. The lady listened and said, I'm sorry, but it will cost you a new hook-up fee to turn it back on; I blew my stack at her and she hung up.

Did they really owe me? I was thinking that because I had so much trouble, they ought to make an exception to their rule. I guess they don't owe me that. It's just that it would have been nice if they did it.

How might I feel if I stopped feeling unjustly treated? I guess I'd just pay the hook-up fee and forget it. Actually, I would have had a lot better day, now that I think about it. I would stop having these fantasies about giving up the cable and writing an angry letter. I don't like the way that makes me feel when I get going like that. It would be a lot better to not feel they owed anything to me except the cable service in exchange for my payment.

Your example 1:

_____

_____

_____

_____

What did they really owe me?

_____

_____

_____

_____

How might I feel if I stopped feeling unjustly treated?

_____

_____

_____

_____

Your example 2:

_____

_____

_____

_____

What did they really owe me?

_____

_____

_____

_____

How might I feel if I stopped feeling unjustly treated?

_____

_____

_____

_____

Your example 3:

_____

_____

_____

_____

What did they really owe me?

_____

_____

_____

_____

How might I feel if I stopped feeling unjustly treated?

_____

_____

_____

_____

This lesson is concentrated on the way you give yourself permission to be angry. The key element that allows you to be angry and become aggressive is your sense that an injustice has occurred. This element is present even when you blow up suddenly. A remark that sets you off or an interruption while you're busy feels like an injustice.

Your anger results from a habit of viewing the world, and others in it, as being obligated to not bother you. The important thing for you to learn is that there is no agreement like that. Most of your problems are not related to someone's failure to treat you in a way that you had earned. You are just in the habit of taking for granted that others owe things to you that they actually do not owe.

Practice Record For Lesson 5

The more you practice recognizing what is not owed to you, the more self-reliant you will become and the less angry you will feel. Keep track for a while of the times you are able to turn anger into self-reliance by recognizing your feeling that an injustice was done when there really wasn't any injustice. Practice seeing that you are owed a lot less than you assume.

Later we will work on cultivating gratitude, but for now enjoy the feeling of taking responsibility for your own happiness.

Keep track of your successes by writing them down in your private notebook. The examples will show you how to arrange your recordings and help get you started. Leave space in your notebook for recording at least five successes.

Example 1: Date: 8/22

Incident: I was reading the paper and my five-year-old jumped on the couch next to me. I felt a flash of anger—more like irritation, really. I was able to think clearly for once and realized that my first response was that he shouldn't have done that. Why not? Because he interrupted me. But why is he obligated to not interrupt me? I will feel a lot better about being a parent if I can stop assuming that my children have a duty not to distract me.

Example 2: Date: 9/1

Incident: I saw an article in the paper saying that the electric company planned to raise their rates. I got really mad at first, as I do a lot about the news. Then I saw that my first reaction was the feeling that they shouldn't do that. All of a sudden it was easy for me to see that I was troubling myself about something I don't even know anything about. I don't know what the electric company is obligated to do about rates. I don't even know how much extra it's going to cost me. I decided to wait and see what change it makes to my electric bill, and then if it's a problem I'll try to figure out what to do.

Lesson 6:
Criticisms and Judgments Keep Anger Warm

Anger isn't stored in our minds like fat stores fuel in our bodies. Anger is a behavior, and it is stored like all behaviors, as a habit. The reason it seems as if our anger is "in us," like potential energy waiting to exert itself, is that when we think certain thoughts or encounter certain events, our readiness to behave in an angry way appears without our bidding.

But, consider, when you encounter something scary, say a creature in a horror film, doesn't fear appear without your bidding? The same is true of something funny. You laugh when you see something funny. Do you carry fear and laughter around with you? If you aren't scared for a while and don't laugh for a while, do fear and laughter build up to the point where they must be "let out" or they will just make you crazy? Doesn't it work the other way around?

If you don't laugh for a long while, it becomes harder to see funny things.

If you are in the habit of laughing at many things in life, then you will laugh a lot. Similarly, if you are in the habit of attacking many things in life, then you will be angry a lot.

If you have an anger problem, you keep your anger alive by practicing it in many ways.

The two major ways you are likely to practice anger are:

• You think critical thoughts or openly criticize on a regular basis.
• You think judgmentally or openly judge on a regular basis.

Taking judgmental thinking first, we know that judgments are a necessary part of life. They come down to calling a spade, a spade. "It's time to get up" is a judgment. "She is my friend" is a judgment. "She is my enemy" is a judgment. Judgments say:

"You are X."

Judgmental thinking adds something to judgments. Judgmental thinking adds a message:

"You are guilty of being X."

Consider the judgments: "Sally plots against me. She is my enemy." You might think that these statements or thoughts can only imply that Sally is guilty of something and therefore they must be judgmental thinking. But they could be either judgmental or factual, and it makes a big difference which way you mean them.

• A guilty judgment implies that someone did something they shouldn't have done and should be punished for it or otherwise be made responsible.
• A factual judgment is only a statement of fact.

An example of a thought that is a guilty judgment is: "Sally plots against me. She is my enemy. I'll fix her. I will not ask her to my party." An example of a thought that is a factual judgment is: "Sally plots against me. She is my enemy. I don't think I'd better ask her to come to my party. I'll just be uncomfortable with her there."

Read these two examples out loud. Notice you are inclined to raise your voice when you read the guilty-judgment example. It is more comfortable to read the factual-judgment example in a calm and matter-of-fact tone. The feeling that accompanies judgments is your best clue as to whether they are judgmental thinking or factual judgments.

Judgmental thinking keeps anger alive and ready. It is a short skip from thinking, "Those people are nuts. Something should be done about them," to verbal attacks, or even more serious attacks on people who are like "those people."

Remember: Avoiding judgmental thinking doesn't mean you can't make factual judgments.

Exercise 6-A: Turning Your Judgmental Thinking Into Factual Thinking

Think of four things, events, groups, or persons that you do not have very good feelings about. Identify some judgmental thinking you do about each one and describe it. Notice how you feel while you write these down and reread them. Then write down factual judgments that you can use to replace your judgmental thinking. Reread your factual judgments and see how you feel. Revise the statements until you can read them without feeling angry.

These two examples will get you started:

Example 1: I think government employees are a bunch of power-hungry leeches who work very little and make us pay the bill.

Factual judgments: Well, I guess the facts are that government employees are often in a position where they carry out some rule, and for some of them it goes to their heads. They tend to get paid pretty well and their pay comes from taxes that I pay. But I guess they pay taxes too.

I still get a twinge of anger reading this. So here goes again.

Revision, if needed: Some government employees have an inflated sense of power. This is likely to irritate people. They are paid with taxes that we all pay, including them.

I can read this more calmly.

Example 2: My ex-husband is a jerk. He's a liar and a deadbeat father. He was a lousy father and a lousy husband.

This is difficult.

Factual judgments: My ex lies and can't be trusted. He neglects the children. He spent his paychecks on toys and drinking when we were married. He tries to get away with paying less child support than he owes.

I feel a little less angry when I read my attempt to make factual judgments, but still feel anger. So I'll try again.

Revision, if needed: My ex tells lies, so I can't trust him. His money support is undependable. That feels better when I read it and think it. It gives me a sense of release. I have to just get on with what I need to do.

Your example 1:

_____

_____

_____
_____
_____

Factual judgments:

_____
_____
_____
_____
_____

Revision, if needed:

_____
_____
_____
_____
_____

Your example 2:

_____
_____
_____
_____
_____

Factual judgments:

_____
_____
_____
_____
_____

Revision, if needed:

_____

_____

_____

_____

_____

Your example 3:

_____

_____

_____

_____

_____

Factual judgments:

_____

_____

_____

_____

_____

Revision, if needed:

_____

_____

_____

_____

_____

Your example 4:

_____

_____

_____

_____

_____

Factual judgments:

_____

_____

_____

_____

_____

Revision, if needed:

_____

_____

_____

_____

_____

Critical thoughts also keep your anger warm and ready to boil over into angry feelings, angry words, and angry actions. If you recognize your critical thoughts and see them as just another form of judgmental thinking, you can free yourself from this source of anger in your life. As with judgments, some thoughts can be matters of fact, not criticisms.

The test of whether a thought is a criticism or a matter of fact is:

Does your thinking lead to more thoughts of how the other person should change, or does it lead to thoughts about what, if anything, you should do?

For example, "That driver is going too slowly," can be a matter of fact, as if you are a driving instructor pointing out something to a student. When you think of it as a matter of fact, your response might be, "Is there something I need to look out for? Maybe I should put on my flashers so someone will not run into me as I slow down."

But a thought such as, "That driver is going too slowly," can also be a criticism that serves to keep your anger warmed up. "That driver is going too slowly. That guy thinks he owns the road."

If your thoughts focus on the behavior of the other person and how the person should change, then it's criticism, it's anger, and it's not good for you.

Examples of Critical Thoughts Versus Factual Thinking

Critical Thoughts	Factual Thinking
Johnny is swinging his bat too soon at pitches. I don't see why he doesn't listen to my advice.	Johnny is swinging his bat too soon at pitches. I wonder what I can do to help him correct that?
She burned dinner again. It's as if she doesn't care about me.	She burned dinner again. Maybe I could help her with dinner.
He didn't respond when I spoke to him. He just doesn't listen to me.	He didn't respond when I spoke to him. Maybe I will leave him a note.

These examples of critical thoughts all include thinking that continues to concentrate on the other person. Matters of fact start with the same thought, but then change to thinking of constructive action. These are thoughts about matters of fact and facts help solve problems without feeling angry.

- Facts help us decide what to do.
- Critical thoughts help us remember that someone, or some part of the world, doesn't always behave the way we wish.

Exercise 6-B:
Recognizing and Changing Critical Thinking

Try to think of four situations you have been in where things didn't go as you wished. Describe the situations, your thoughts at the time, and decide whether these were critical thinking or just thinking about the facts. If you find they were critical thinking, write down a direction your thoughts could have taken that would have been more factual. These two examples show you what to do.

Example 1: I was out to dinner with my wife and some friends of ours. My wife started talking about something that happened that embarrassed me and I would just as soon not have our friends know about.

My thoughts: I thought, Oh no, she's telling that story. Why is she doing that? Is she trying to embarrass me? She's doing this to get a laugh at my expense.

Was this critical thinking? I guess it was. My thoughts continued about my wife and her behavior and why it was occurring. I also felt angry and we argued later.

Just the facts: My wife was telling a story that embarrassed me. What to do? These were our friends. Did I really need to feel defensive in front of them? It was, after all, a funny story. There is another stupid thing I did that is even funnier. Maybe I'll tell it myself later.

Example 2: I came home and my husband was lying on the couch watching TV. The house was a mess and dinner hadn't been started.

My thoughts: He's watching TV and the house is a mess. He expects me to do everything. He treats me like his mother. She always cleaned up after him and now he expects me to do it.

Was this critical thinking? Well, my thoughts did go on and on about my husband's behavior and what happened. I kept thinking about it all night and I felt distant and irritated with him all evening. Even when we were watching a funny TV show together later, we would laugh. But when the commercial came on, I'd start to think about him sitting there when I came home and the same old thoughts got me irritated again.

Just the facts: I came home and my husband was watching TV and the house was a mess. What can I do? I can ask him to straighten up the house while I get dinner going. Or better yet, we could order in Chinese food and straighten up the house together while we wait for it to be delivered. Then we could watch TV together.

Your example 1:

_____

_____

_____

_____

_____

_____

My thoughts:

_____

_____

_____

_____

_____

_____

Was this critical thinking?

_____

_____

_____

_____

_____

_____

Just the facts:

_____

_____

_____

_____

_____

Your example 2:

_____

_____

_____

_____

_____

My thoughts:

_____

_____

_____

_____

_____

Was this critical thinking?

_____

_____

_____

_____

_____

_____

Just the facts:

_____

_____

_____

_____

_____

_____

Your example 3:

_____

_____

_____

_____

_____

_____

My thoughts:

_____

_____

_____

_____

_____

Was this critical thinking?

_____
_____
_____
_____
_____
_____

Just the facts:

_____
_____
_____
_____
_____
_____

Your example 4:

_____
_____
_____
_____
_____
_____

My thoughts:

_____
_____
_____
_____
_____
_____

Was this critical thinking?

_____

_____

_____

_____

_____

_____

Just the facts:

_____

_____

_____

_____

_____

_____

Critical thoughts and judgmental thinking are habits. They are your habits and therefore you can change them. Changing your judgmental and critical thinking to factual thinking takes practice, but you can do it.

It takes a lot of energy and a pretty good memory to stay angry. Habits of thinking critically and judgmentally make it easier for you to get angry in any situation that comes along and to stay that way. It's like having your car's motor running at all times. The car is ready to take off. Shutting off the anger-habit motor means that you will not rush to anger every time you encounter a problem.

One indication that you have this motor running is knowing that you are angry with someone about something, but you can't remember why or what actually happened. You find yourself trying to remember a person's "offense," so that you can rearouse the feeling of anger. If you weren't feeling angry, why on earth would you look for a reason to be angry?

The answer is that your tendency to be and remain judgmental carries the day, even when the feeling of anger has quieted down. So there is always the unfinished business of someone's guilt and their need to change that serves to reawaken your anger. You remain the enforcer and the critic. These remain on your list. You may have to look up their offense; but you must do your critical and judgmental job.

It will be a gigantic relief to you to give up judgmental and critical thinking. As you learn to be more factual in your thoughts, especially in your judgments, you will find anger less available. You will simply get out of the habit of judging. There is enormous relief in learning to tend your own garden. You become a more satisfied person with whom others are more comfortable and with whom you are more comfortable.

Practice at intercepting your critical thoughts and judgmental thinking is required. It will help you if you keep track of your successes for a while. Record in your private notebook the first five times you are able to intervene in your own critical or judgmental thoughts and make them factual. The examples will show you how to set up your notebook and what to record.

Practice Record For Lesson 6

Example 1: Date: 10/23

Situation and my thoughts: The company I work for is always trying to make some change that everyone knows isn't going to help anything. They started a new procedure where everyone in my department must do a checklist on the condition of the equipment every morning before they begin work. I found myself thinking that these people don't know what they are doing. They just pull things out of their you-know-what.

My success in making my thoughts factual: So I thought, you know, management started this checklist without realizing that maintenance keeps an inspection record of this equipment. I wondered if I mentioned this to my supervisor, if she would straighten this out so either maintenance or we would be doing the inspection, not both. It really felt good to get off the criticism kick.

Example 2: Date: 11/2

Situation and my thoughts: My wife had parked her car behind mine in the driveway. She was still sleeping and I had to get to work. I couldn't find her car keys. I kept thinking how thoughtless my wife is. She only has her mind on what's easiest at the moment. She doesn't think ahead that someone else might need to get out of the driveway.

My success in making my thoughts factual: I reminded myself that my critical thoughts and judgments about my wife were keeping me angry and would probably result in a fight. I decided to stay with the facts, "Just the facts, ma'am." Her car is behind mine. I can't find the keys to move it. They are probably in her purse. This is no big deal. I looked and there they are. I'm going to have a lot better day. And I did.

Lesson 7:
Self-Importance, Anger, and Self-Esteem

A major source of anger is a person's sense of self-importance. Self-importance is quite different from self-esteem. In fact, it is a major barrier to the development of self-esteem. Your self-esteem assures you that you have the ability to deal with whatever occurs in your life with competence and grace. Self-importance leads you to assume that whatever you want or need is owed to you because of who or what you are.

People with high self-importance assume that what they want is owed to them due to the fact that they want it. People with high self-esteem do not hesitate to attempt to earn their way in the world. Nearly everyone has a problem with self-importance, and this is how we get that way. From birth most of us are surrounded by a multitude of things that we didn't earn and didn't arrange—

the air we breathe, the care we are given, the food made available to us, the concern of others about us.

These and a thousand other things are just there, given to us without our having to arrange for them. It is very difficult for us to understand why parents, siblings, teachers, relatives, and a host of others make their help available to us, even their unwelcome attempts to change us. So we are apt to assume it's because we deserve their concern and attention. We deserve everything we get just because we exist, because we are who and what we are.

Another way of putting this is that:
We don't easily see that what we receive is given to us as a gift.

Instead of an attitude of gratitude for what we get from others, we are apt to develop an attitude of entitlement. Two telltale signs of a self-important attitude are:

1. Parent bashing, that is, repetitive criticism of how you were reared and blaming parents for your difficulties.
2. An inability to recognize and accept gifts with a sense of gratitude.

As usual, it is easier to recognize problems in others than in ourselves. So we will start with what you have observed in others. One of three things must be present for a self-important person to accept a "gift." Either they badly need it, in which case they feel they deserve it. Or they insist on paying for it in some way. Or they feel they are owed it because of who they are.

In no case can anyone actually give them a gift.

Perhaps you have had the experience of offering someone a ride home from work, not because they really needed it, but just because you wanted to do it. And then they say something like

"You don't need to do that" or "OK, but I'll catch you later and return the favor" or "Here, I'll give you money for gas." As the giver, you have a sense of emptiness when this happens.

This person just will not accept a gift from you. Either it is paid for in some way, or they declare that it isn't needed. If it were needed, it wouldn't be a gift either. It would be owed to them because they needed it. Their statement, "You don't need to do that" implies that when they need something, that is when *you* need to do it.

There is hardly any more demoralizing existence than to live with someone who will not accept gifts from you. After all, love is a gift, and it must be a gift if it is to be love. Self-important people do not accept gifts. They don't even know what gifts are. Everything must be deserved or it must be paid for. Therefore, to the extent that people are self-important they cannot accept love.

You may give and give and give some more. Yet what is given is not accepted as a gift. It is either accepted as partial payment of what you owe because they deserve it, or is accepted only in exchange for some payment.

Exercise 7-A:
Recognizing Self-Importance in Others

Think of someone you know who either expected something from you because they needed it, or wouldn't accept something from you without promising to pay you back in some way.

These two examples will help you get started.

Example 1: I tried to give my mother a new dress. She said, "I don't need that. You are just wasting your money. I don't see how I can get you a present like that." It's funny, but she also complains a lot about not having things. She often makes my life miserable with her complaints about her car. She didn't even say thank you when I had her car fixed one time. I never thought of her before as being self-important.

Example 2: My teenage daughter gets all bent out of shape when some friend of hers gets something new. She must have one just like it or she will just die. She doesn't exactly beg. She goes into this sullen mood, demonstrating at every opportunity how unhappy she is. If I get it for her, she's happy for a little bit, but doesn't thank me. She just acts as if she's been freed from a state of oppression. My wife says she's spoiled. Now that I think about it, being spoiled is kind of like self-importance.

Your example 1:

_____

_____

_____

_____

_____

Your example 2:

_____

_____

_____

_____

_____

Your example 3:

_____

_____

_____

_____

_____

Perhaps now that you begin to see self-importance in others, you may begin to see it in yourself. Can you accept gifts from others? Or do gifts make you feel obligated? When you feel you need help, do you ask for help and accept a refusal of help with grace? Or do you resent it and get angry when others will not help you?

Self-importance and anger go together in adults like spoiled children and whining. Parent-bashing is likely to be leftover self-importance from childhood. It is encouraged by our cultural view that parenting is an obligation rather than an expression of love. We assume that parents take responsibility for their children's welfare because they must do so. Someone who loves you isn't *obligated* to care for you. Love is voluntary, and to view it otherwise kills both love and gratitude. Your parents did what they could for you out of love, not because they had to.

You will be enormously relieved if and when you are able to cultivate an attitude of gratitude toward your parents and others who have helped you. Much of your anger will dissipate, and you will put down a heavy burden. The burden is your resentment and unhappiness resulting from feeling that you haven't received all that you deserved.

Exercise 7-B:
Identifying Your Own Self-Importance

Think of five recent incidents where you became irritated or angry when someone didn't respond to what you felt you wanted or needed. These two examples will get you started.

Example 1: I was at work and this young kid who works there made a smart remark directed at me. It irritated me and it kept coming back into my thoughts all day. I kept thinking of things I wish I'd said that would have really put him in his place. I think the remark irritated me because he was treating me like one of his teenage friends. I'm older and feel as if I'm above that sort of thing. I guess that means that I expect treatment that puts me above his ordinary place in life.

Example 2: I was shopping for a car and I had my gardening clothes on. I noticed the salesman kind of sized me up as I came into the showroom. He continued to talk on the phone while I looked at some expensive cars on the showroom floor. I began to boil. I was thinking things like telling him I had been ready to pay cash for the $45,000 car on the floor, but changed my mind because of his example of how I would be treated there. Or, better yet, I'd tell his manager the same thing. I see that it was just my self-importance that was offended by his neglect. He was judging me by my clothes. I wanted him to automatically treat me as special. Maybe that's why I wanted such an expensive car in the first place.

Your example 1:

_____

_____

_____

_____

_____

Your example 2:

_____

_____

_____

_____

_____

Your example 3:

_____
_____
_____
_____
_____

Your example 4:

_____
_____
_____
_____
_____

Your example 5:

_____
_____
_____
_____
_____

The biggest reward for giving up self-importance is the opportunity to develop self-esteem. Self-esteem is not compatible with self-importance. Your self-esteem consists of confidence that whatever happens to you, you will deal with it in a way you will feel good about.

Self-importance assumes that what happens to you depends on other people treating you in the way you are entitled to be treated. Self-importance makes you a "nervous Nellie" who must observe what others think of you and is apt to get angry with people who don't recognize your entitlements. Self-esteem makes you a "confident Nellie" who accepts what is given gratefully, and pursues what is not given with self-assurance. Changing self-importance to self-esteem calms you down and you get angry much less easily.

Anger is always involved in control. When you need not trouble yourself with whether or not other people see you as worthy of their deference, then you need not try to control how others see you.

Converting your self-importance to self-esteem will be aided by always being ready to ask one question: Do I want to attend to how others view me, or would I rather concentrate on what I'm doing?

For example, if you are shopping, do you want to pay attention to how the salespeople view you, or do you want to concentrate on the merchandise and whether it suits you? If you are a student, do you want to concentrate on how other students and teachers view you, or do you want to concentrate on the subject matter you're learning? If you are a homeowner, do you want to be concerned with how others view your house, or do you want to be concerned with whether it suits your needs and is properly maintained?

Being able to work at what you want wholeheartedly, without feeling on stage in front of those around you, is the outcome of substituting self-esteem for self-importance.

Exercise 7-C:
Identifying What You Want

Think of the areas of your life, your family, your work, and your amusements. Identify three things you want in one or more of these areas and then look carefully for something you do self-consciously, as if you are performing for others. Write how you can decrease your self-importance and increase your self-esteem by "getting off the stage" and just concentrating on what you want.

These two examples will help you see what to do.

Example 1: When I go out with my friends to play softball or just sitting around drinking and talking, I get it into my head that I have to be concerned about how they look at me. I do and say stuff that makes me really self-conscious. And then I get angry and hurt when someone mimics me.

How I can decrease my self-importance and increase my self-esteem: I've always been aware of this behavior and have tried to stop it. Now I see that my attempts to stop it have just been efforts to act more effectively in front of my friends. I see now that what I can do is stop trying to stop, and instead concentrate on what I want. If I want to play well, concentrate on the ball. If I want to make people laugh, concentrate on remembering a really good joke. I just want to have a good time. I don't need to perform for them.

Example 2: I want my wife to love me. I'm always trying to imagine how she is viewing me. She keeps saying I should just be myself. And then I try to imagine how that might look, and then I do and say some pretty stupid things. My wife teases me and mocks me and it really upsets me.

How I can decrease my self-importance and increase my self-esteem: I think I get it now. I need to stop concentrating on all this stuff and stop worrying about her loving me. Instead, I need to pay attention to what I'm doing and just try to do it the way I want to do it. I've always wanted a garden. I think I'll start one.

Your example 1:

_____

_____

_____

_____

_____

How I can decrease my self-importance and increase my self-esteem:

_____

_____

_____

_____

_____

Your example 2:

_____

_____

_____

_____

_____

How I can decrease my self-importance and increase my self-esteem:

_____

_____

_____

_____

_____

Your example 3:

_____

_____

_____

_____

_____

How I can decrease my self-importance and increase my self-esteem:

_____

_____

_____

_____

_____

_____

Self-esteem is a valuable prize. Its cost is your self-importance. With self-esteem comes, at no extra cost, fewer occasions for attempting to control others. That will make you calmer and less angry. As with all valuable change in your life, you need to practice, practice, and practice. It helps to keep a record of successes when you are attempting change, so use your private notebook to keep track of some successes in overcoming self-importance in favor of self-esteem.

These examples will show you how to set up your record.

Practice Record For Lesson 7

Example 1: Date: 1/10

Incident: When I was working my way up in the company, it seemed as if I never took myself too seriously. Now I have a very responsible job and a rather high income. My wife kept telling me that I'd changed. I didn't believe her until I started thinking about self-importance. I think I've gotten more concerned about how others view me. It's as if I earned people's respect by doing a good job at work, and now my job has changed into convincing people that I deserve their respect. There's a big difference between trying to do a good job like I was doing before, and trying to look as if I'm doing a good job, like I seem to be doing now.

What I did: I sat down with my wife and told her what I thought has happened. She helped remind me of the things I worked on and what I did to be successful, and I began to remember what those days were like. Solving real problems, studying and learning, writing plans for the department; these were the things I really enjoyed and I'm good at. I had self-esteem at one time and lost it when I became important. I'm going to try to get back to focusing on what I can do for the company. If I can't find my way back to doing that, my wife and I discussed going elsewhere, maybe starting over.

Example 2: Date: 1/20

Incident: I was in a restaurant waiting for a table. My wife and I had a drink while we were waiting. We waited so long I had two drinks, and I began to get angry watching people who had come in after us being seated. My wife tried to calm me down, but I kept complaining, and I guess I was getting kind of loud.

What I did: It occurred to me that we had come into the restaurant happy and expecting to have a good time. Now I was angry and on the verge of having an argument with my wife. What went wrong? I realized that what had set me off was that others were getting seated; and I took for granted it was because they were considered more important than we were. Then I said to myself, "Has it come to this—where a host in a restaurant can make our evening miserable by not treating me as if I'm important?" The pressure went out of my anger and I told my wife what I was thinking. We joked about being unimportant to a waiter. This led to a discussion that lasted all evening about what things are important to us and how we can concentrate on them.

Lesson 8:
Anger and Lack of Communication in Relationships

Anger and good communication don't mix. Anger is about control. Communication is about facts. Anger chooses its words according to whether they will have a controlling effect. Communication chooses its words according to whether they tell the truth. When anger is present, even the truth is suspect.

It is not unusual for couples in counseling to have come to the point where if one says "It's going to be a nice day," the other thinks, "What is she after me to do, clean the rain gutters?" They are at the point where continual angry interaction has made communication—even about the weather forecast—impossible.

Communication suffers as a result of anger in all relationships. Management people and laborers, once they become angry, view everything that's said by the other as an attempt to manipulate, not communicate. Friends, once they start fighting, trust only the attempts of the other person to hurt them. Neighbors who are angry cannot agree on the most obvious facts. If the one neighbor said it, the other feels it's a distortion.

In order to break through anger in a relationship and reestablish communication, it is helpful to understand that relationship anger expresses itself by accusations of being victimized.

This means that verbal fights are almost always about making the other side admit that you are a bigger victim than they are. A marital fight, for instance, might go like this:

Andy: "You really embarrassed me at that party." (Andy's claim that Sally has hurt him.)

Sally: "Nothing I ever say is good enough for you." (Sally's claim that Andy hurts her more often than she hurts him.)

Andy: "You're always saying that. You make me out to be some kind of monster." (Andy counters with a wider claim of being hurt by Sally.)

Sally: "Well, maybe you ought to try living with someone you can't trust." (Sally ups the ante with an allusion to Andy's behavior with other women and reclaims her standing as the one who has the bigger cross to bear.)

This example of escalating claims of being more hurt and injured is typical of relationship anger, regardless of whether it's between individuals, groups, institutions, or countries. So you probably have some experience with this kind of thing and are probably quite good at it.

The winner at this "game" is the one that can claim the biggest hurt. The "game" often ends with someone getting so emotional and out of control that they do or say something really reprehensible. They are then immediately the loser, and the other party gets a free pass to injure at will.

Notice that there is no statement in Sally and Andy's escalating fight that is likely to be entirely true. We are not talking about truth in some philosophical and problematic sense. "Truth" here means the ordinary way we all know well. Are you lying and distorting or telling the truth? In this everyday sense, truth is the first requirement for communication and is rarely found in arguments.

In the example, Andy's initial proclamation that Sally embarrassed him is the closest to a statement of fact. If he had said, "I felt embarrassed when you said…" it would have been factual and would have qualified as communication (assuming Sally said what Andy said she had).

Reestablishing communication in a relationship begins with substituting factual statements for claims that the other person has hurt you. For example, instead of "You embarrassed me" you could substitute "I felt embarrassed when that happened."

The best place to begin practicing substituting facts for claims of hurt made while you are arguing is in your imagination. This is because you are likely to think of starting an argument several times for every time you actually launch one. So you will have lots of opportunities to change the statements in your head.

Exercise 8-A:
Replacing Angry Language with Communication

Think of five ways arguments begin in your relationships with others. Write down the charges you have made against others while arguing. Then change what you have written into something factual.

Helpful Hint: Treat any statement with "always" or "never" in it as not factual.

The following two examples of argument starters will help you determine what to do.

Example 1: My girlfriend and I were bowling and we got in an argument like we always do. She irritated me by laughing when I missed an easy shot. I stewed for a while. And then she asked me what was wrong with me. That really made me mad. I thought, "There's nothing wrong with me. What's wrong with you? You're always finding things about me to put down and laugh at."

Make the argument starter into a communication starter: Well, I guess after I calmed down I could have said that I didn't feel very good when she laughed at me. It seems like a silly thing, but sometimes it feels like she pulls back from being my friend. Hey, now that I think of it, maybe we need to talk about how we react to what we say to each other.

Example 2: My husband John is really tough on the kids. He comes home and everyone is tense because they know it's only a matter of time until he screams at one of them for not doing something just right. Our arguments about this usually start with my saying something like, "For heaven's sake, John, leave them alone. They're scared of you as it is. Do you want them to hate you?"

Make the argument starter into a communication starter: To tell the truth, John's relationship with the kids scares me. I'm afraid of what it's doing to him and his relationship with the children. I think he's also scared about what will happen to the kids because he thinks I'm too soft on them. Maybe that's what I could say. Something like, "John, I think we are both concerned about the kids. I worry about them not being as close to you as they were. I think maybe you worry about how I treat them."

Your example 1:

_____

_____

_____

_____

_____

Make the argument starter into a communication starter:

_____

_____

_____

_____

_____

Your example 2:

_____

_____

_____

_____

_____

Make the argument starter into a communication starter:

_____

_____

_____

_____

_____

Your example 3:

_____

_____

_____

_____

_____

_____

Make the argument starter into a communication starter:

_____

_____

_____

_____

_____

_____

Your example 4:

_____

_____

_____

_____

_____

_____

Make the argument starter into a communication starter:

_____

_____

_____

_____

_____

_____

Your example 5:

_____

_____

_____

_____

_____

_____

Make the argument starter into a communication starter:

_____

_____

_____

_____

_____

_____

Relationship arguments are a form of competition. Usually the competition is to see who can claim control by demonstrating that they have the biggest complaint. Every form of head-to-head competition requires the "players" to hold back information from their "opponents."

You don't play poker by telling others what cards you hold. If anything, you try to mislead other players. In basketball you don't always dribble to the right and then shoot. Your opponents can guard you easily if they know what you're up to. Football has many forms of deception, from trap blocking to reverses. All competitions and all conflicts involve deception and intelligence gathering.

Communication can't stand deception. Its "rules" are just the opposite of competition. The more open the lines of communication are, the better the quality of communication is. The more closed and deceptive the lines of communication between competitors are, the better the quality of competition is.

- Deception drives out communication.
- Deception feeds conflict.
- Good communication requires trust.

The good things that come out of good relationships result from trust. Even third graders, when they are trying to establish a friendship will start by telling a classmate a secret, a small one at first. Then, if the other child is receptive to friendship, they will tell a secret in return.

The children are then on their way to a trusting relationship that allows them to be vulnerable to one another. The information they share could easily be used to attack one another, and sometimes it is, ending the relationship abruptly.

Some view arguments and fighting as healthy for relationships, providing that the fighting stays within certain boundaries. The best rules are: don't lie, don't exaggerate, and don't humiliate. In other words, don't fight.

If a good relationship requires trust, then whatever makes either party untrustworthy will harm the relationship to some degree. Making yourself into "the one who suffers the most" in order to try to win an argument and win control over another person requires the stealth and cunning of a good defense lawyer. It requires a certain amount of exaggeration, misrepresentation, and misdirection. All these "skills" serve to undermine communication.

Adversarial proceedings, such as those that take place in the legal system, are not exercises in finding the truth. They are exercises in finding blame. Adversarial proceedings in relationships, likewise, are undertaken in order to find blame. If and when blame is found, then the guilty party must repent. It is the repentance of the other party that each participant seeks. Real communication, truth, and intimacy are casualties of angry exchanges.

Exercise 8-B: Understanding Why You Argue with Family and Friends

Recall three arguments you have had with others among your family and friends. Describe the issue in each case and then ask yourself why you argued with the other person. That is, why did you carry out the argument, not why did you believe what you did? What were you trying to accomplish by arguing? Then consider a more friendly approach to what you were trying to accomplish that doesn't require making someone into an adversary.

These two examples will help you get the idea of what to do.

Example 1: My wife and I argued over money as usual. I tried to convince her that she couldn't just keep charging things. We already took out a home equity loan on the house in order to pay down credit cards. Now they are run up again. The argument got rather heated and we have hardly spoken since.

What was I trying to accomplish? I guess I was trying to get my wife to stop charging things on our credit cards. Really that means spending less. I'm not sure why she spends as much as she does, so I guess I was trying to change her behavior without knowing a lot about it. Change her behavior—sounds like I was trying to take control of her behavior. Even if I could win an argument with her about money, it probably wouldn't change her behavior.

What's a more friendly approach? This is difficult. Maybe the approach I was taking was really to try to worry my wife as much as I'm worried about money. Trying to make her worry might not be a good idea. She already knows everything about our situation that I do. Maybe she's already worried and just doesn't want to get more alarmed than she is already. My coming at her can't be very pleasant then. Maybe I could start there. I'll tell her I'm worried and ask her for help. Maybe she would open up and we could really talk about what we can do and help each other to get through this.

Example 2: A friend of mine made a snide remark about someone who is a close friend of mine. I told her I thought her remark wasn't fair. She got all hurt and said if that's the way I felt then she guessed we couldn't be friends anymore. I tried to tell her that wasn't true and I wasn't criticizing her, I just didn't want to hear her criticism of this other person. She said, "Well, we'll have to see," and she's been rather cold ever since then.

What was I trying to accomplish? She made me mad when she put my close friend down. I felt I needed to defend my friend. What did I accomplish? Well, I guess I was trying to make her feel uncomfortable for having said what she said. After all, I called her remark "unfair." I guess it's true that I was trying to punish her. But I don't want to lose her as a friend. Oh my—what I was doing really doesn't make much sense to me now.

What's a more friendly approach? Well, I'm certainly not going to agree with criticism of my friends just to keep from offending someone. "Agree to disagree," I guess that's the point. I didn't really need to criticize her by saying she was being unfair. I could have just said that the person she made the remark about is a good friend and I didn't agree. I could have kept it friendly. I'm sure we wouldn't have argued and she wouldn't have been offended if I hadn't said something critical of what she said. Maybe I can talk to her and say just that. I'm sorry I called her remark unfair. I should have just said I didn't agree with her on that. We agree on most other things.

Your example 1:

_____
_____
_____
_____
_____

What was I trying to accomplish?

_____
_____
_____
_____
_____

What's a more friendly approach?

_____
_____
_____
_____
_____

Your example 2:

_____
_____
_____
_____

What was I trying to accomplish?

_____
_____
_____

_____

_____

What's a more friendly approach?

_____

_____

_____

_____

_____

Your example 3:

_____

_____

_____

_____

_____

What was I trying to accomplish?

_____

_____

_____

_____

_____

What's a more friendly approach?

_____

_____

_____

_____

_____

Substituting communication for argument can have important effects on your life. It may save your marriage. It certainly will contribute to a more rational and calm approach to your life. Perhaps the most important effect is that it opens the door to friendship and intimacy.

As long as you remain ready to argue with others, you will need to be prepared for battle. A natural part of remaining ready for battle is to keep secrets.

It isn't just "important" secrets that you keep. Like the Defense Department, when you're not sure what use can be made of some information, it tends to get stamped "secret." You become less communicative and more argumentative. Both wear down your friendships and intimate relationships. Friends and intimates have no Freedom of Information Act with which to require disclosure of your thoughts.

Becoming less argumentative and more communicative takes lots of practice. It is helpful to keep a record of your success in heading off the tendency to be guarded with your thoughts.

Turning *preparations to argue* into *preparations to communicate* is also helpful.

Use your private notebook to keep a record of your successes for a while. The examples will show you how to set up your pages and help get you started.

Practice Record For Lesson 8

Example 1: Date: 2/15

Success: This guy at work is always making some provocative remark to see if he can get a rise out of me. Yesterday he said, "You must not be able to find a better job, or you wouldn't be working in a place like this." I almost took the bait and then I caught myself. I don't need to argue with him. He's just a bitter guy who isn't very happy. So I said to him, "I'm sorry you feel that way." And went back to work. Last night, I was telling my husband about this and he said he noticed I was in a good mood when I got home. We had a nice talk.

Example 2: Date: 2/22

Success: My wife suggested that we go to a different place next year for a vacation. My first impulse was to argue with her about it. We've been going to the same place every year for ten years. I caught myself and thought, "How can I make this into a discussion rather than an argument?" So I asked myself what my real reactions to the idea were. I felt a little frightened.

We would have to find out how to make new arrangements. We wouldn't know the place. Really, these all come down to the same thing—it scares me. So I said to her, "The idea scares me." And she said it scares her too. Then we started a really good discussion of why we are in such a rut. We've continued the discussion since, and I feel as if we are on the same team for the first time in a long time. It isn't as hard to think about doing new things if we feel like we can help each other.

Lesson 9:
Reducing Anxiety by Giving Up the Social Rejection Game

Perhaps you have experienced performance anxiety when you were preparing to give a speech or perform in front of an audience. Maybe the audience is made up of people you know and feel comfortable with, but you have anxiety when you are getting ready to talk to them all together.

What's the difference between talking to people all together and talking with them individually that would make you feel anxiety?

When you are talking to people individually, they respond, and you are able to correct and guide what you say with some sense that you know how your audience is responding to you. You can monitor and control how individuals, taken a few at a time, think about you. You have a sense that you can keep from making a fool of yourself. But when talking to a group, you are unable to keep track of their individual responses to you.

If you have the need to control other people's responses to you, the job becomes unmanageable when people are in a group. This is frightening to you.

Therefore, your attempts to control others are likely to become a source of anxiety for you. What is commonly called social anxiety results from being unsure you can control the responses of others when you are either in a new situation or in a social situation with too many people for you to monitor. You may say, "But I don't want to control anyone. I just don't want them thinking badly of me."

But ask yourself: **Why do critical thoughts that others have matter to me?**

Surely you are not perfect, so there are always going to be things that someone else can criticize. Ask any politician if that isn't true. Consider that the reason you feel you need to avoid critical thoughts from others is that you are used to competing with others for social advantages using faultlessness as a kind of currency. Others' faults entitle you to social superiority. And your faults entitle you to social scorn and rejection.

Products and their usefulness to consumers settle competition as to which has the better widget, or who is the better surgeon. Gossip, reputation, and appearance tend to settle competition for social control in families, groups, and small communities. This kind of competition uses criticism and moral judgments as weapons.

Like any other kind of competition, if you play, you play by the rules. And the rules say that if you are the object of scornful mockery, you lose. Your acceptance of social rejection is the feeling of shame. In order to keep from losing—and subsequently scorned and shamed—you will need to monitor how you appear to all the other players, anticipate their rejection, and change your behavior or what you are saying accordingly. Regardless of how confident they look, all of the other players in the social rejection game are doing the same thing.

If you don't play, then the rules are meaningless, and the scorn of others is just their useless expended energy. At the same time, you will need to learn to live without the prospect of feeling superior to others and being critical of them.

Exercise 9-A: Recognize When You're Competing For Social Control

---

When your anxiety is accompanied by thoughts about how others will respond to you, it's a good clue that you are "in the game." You are likely to be competing for a position above other people's social rejection and from which you can criticize others.

Choose three times you have felt anxiety leading to some event. Try to remember what you were thinking. Write down the anxiety incident along with the thoughts you were having. Were they thoughts about how others might respond to you? Were you concerned about their scorn, their disrespect? Do you disrespect or socially reject others?

These two examples of anxiety incidents will help you get started:

Example 1: I was going to meet my boyfriend's family. I could hardly sleep the night before. I felt really anxious, almost to the point of panic.

My thoughts: That's why I couldn't sleep. I kept imagining all kinds of things, such as what the situation would look like and what they would say. I imagined them stern and I imagined them warm. I imagined his mother stern and his father warm. And I imagined them the other way around. I tried to imagine how I would act and what I would say. All this got me even more wound up.

Was I concerned about social rejection? Of course I was. I didn't want my boyfriend's family thinking I'm not good enough for him. I guess I imagine that others are judging me a lot. Sort of like when I was in school and girls formed cliques and talked about other girls and laughed about them. I always hated that, but I wanted to be included in a clique anyway.

Do I socially reject others in this way? I guess I do. I certainly talk about others sometimes in ways that I know would hurt them if they heard about it. It makes me feel bad about myself when I do that. Now that I think about it, the way I imagine that they would feel if they knew I said those things is what I was feeling when I was imagining how my boyfriend's family might react to me. Ouch!

Example 2: My husband is a doctor and we attend dinners at a lot of the other doctors' houses. I put off giving a dinner party as long as I could, but I just had to do a payback. I was a wreck. I thought of nothing else for two weeks before and had trouble sleeping.

My thoughts: I thought of a million things. Everything from how the lawn looked to the paint that is chipping on the basement stairs. Everywhere I looked I could see how someone might notice something wrong. The worst part was I knew that none of them would say anything to me about it. And I wouldn't know what they were saying to each other later.

Was I concerned about social rejection? Of course I was. I know how those people talk. Lots of time in the past I felt really anxious when someone would mention something critical about someone's housekeeping and I knew that my house was worse than that.

Do I socially reject others in this way? I like to feel that I respect everyone. But I know that's not really true. The worse thing is, I want to be part of the group that's envied by others. That makes me feel that I want to be superior. I guess I do participate in conversations that are critical of others.

Your example 1:

_____
_____
_____
_____
_____
_____

My thoughts:

_____
_____
_____
_____
_____

Was I concerned about social rejection?

_____
_____
_____
_____
_____

Do I socially reject others in this way?

_____

_____

_____

_____

_____

_____

Your example 2:

_____

_____

_____

_____

_____

_____

My thoughts:

_____

_____

_____

_____

_____

_____

Was I concerned about social rejection?

_____

_____

_____

_____

_____

_____

Do I socially reject others in this way?

_____
_____
_____
_____
_____
_____

Your example 3:

_____
_____
_____
_____
_____
_____

My thoughts:

_____
_____
_____
_____
_____
_____

Was I concerned about social rejection?

_____
_____
_____
_____
_____

Do I socially reject others in this way?

_____

_____

_____

_____

_____

_____

You have two choices if you wish to reduce your anxiety in social and performance situations:

1. You can aspire to perfection, or
2. You can stop participating in the social rejection game.

Probably no amount of perfection will ever really insulate you from the possibility of criticism and scorn from others. But you can change your habit of jockeying for superior status. This will allow you to give up your tendency to monitor others and yourself for vulnerability to social rejection. If you find it worthwhile to continue to evaluate others in a scornful and rejecting manner, you will naturally feel like a potential target for that same treatment coming back at you from others.

Others cannot humiliate you socially if you don't let them. In adult life, as in junior high school, cliques are self-proclaimed, and the rules for belonging are vague and volatile. They aren't like the Elks or an alumni association. When you join organizations with charters and bylaws, you might be on probation for a while, but once you are in, you are in.

Except in countries that still have blood-defined nobility or caste systems, social superiority is never permanent. It is always probationary. You may be in today, but you are always subject to expulsion tomorrow.

If you wish to be in a position to be scornful of others, you will always be on social probation.

Your probationary status drives your social and performance anxiety. Just about anyone can become your self-appointed probation officer, and with a scornful flourish revoke your membership in the group of those who assume a position from which they can be scornful of others. They're just not minding their own business.

Exercise 9-B:
How To Get Off "Social Probation"

Leaving behind a life of imaginary scrutiny by others is difficult. It requires that you give up something that may be very dear to you, namely your desire to be admired. Some people may admire you in some ways, but you can never achieve the unconditional status of permanent admiration.

Facing this means you must come squarely to grips with the hard fact that the meaning of your life is too valuable to put into the hands of just anyone who happens along. And most important, the meaning of other people's lives is too valuable to be demeaned by your limited, passing view of their behaviors. If you are seeking a friend, by all means make a judgment as to whether a person is suitable as your friend. But don't go beyond that. If you are looking for an honest person to confide in, by all means make a judgment as to whether you feel you can trust that person, but don't go beyond that.

Try examining your views of other people you know at work, in your family, and socially. Find someone you have been scornful of in each of these areas of your life. Write down your views of them. Then ask yourself: "What has this to do with me?" Shave off all your criticism except how their lives affect yours. Then ask yourself:

"If others had these same criticisms of you, what would these 'defects' have to do with their lives?"

These two examples will help you see how this plays out.

Views of person I'm critical of at work

Example 1: Joe works in my building. He's crude, very over-weight, and kind of dumb. Our nickname for him is "Dumbo."

What has this criticism to do with my life? Well, nothing I guess. Joe seems to do his job. He isn't a friend; he doesn't seem to have any friends.

What would these same criticisms, leveled at me by others, have to do with their lives? I see what this is about now. Just as my snide remarks are about things that really aren't my business, if someone else had these opinions of me, they would be critical of something that wasn't their business. I worry about what others think of how I come across, but I see that whatever they think, however I come across, doesn't affect them anyway. They're just being nasty busybodies.

Views of person I'm critical of in my family

Example 2: My mother-in-law has always been a laughing stock for me and my brothers-in law. She's a dizzy dame who gets things wrong most of the time. She goes on and on about things and doesn't know what she's talking about most of the time. Sometimes she gets things exactly opposite of what they really are.

What has the criticism to do with my life? I guess it comes down to that sometimes she passes messages on incorrectly. But I take account of that. She puts out a lot of wrong information, but then I also take that into account. I guess the way she is really isn't any of my business.

What would these same criticisms, leveled at me by others, have to do with their lives? If someone thinks I'm dizzy and laughs at me behind my back, they are really going beyond anything that affects them. Why would they do it even if I didn't keep things straight? I guess I can grow up and stop criticizing people whose faults don't affect me. Maybe I can also stop worrying about what others think of me if they aren't any more grown up than I have been.

Views of person I'm critical of at work

Your example 1:

_____

_____

_____

_____

_____

_____

What has the criticism to do with my life?

_____

_____

_____

_____

_____

_____

What would these same criticisms, leveled at me by others, have to do with their lives?

_____

_____

_____

_____

_____

_____

_____

Views of person I'm critical of in my family

Your example 2:

_____

_____

_____

_____

_____

_____

What has the criticism to do with my life?

_____

_____

_____

_____

_____

_____

What would these same criticisms, leveled at me by others, have to do with their lives?

_____

_____

_____

_____

_____

_____

Views of person I'm critical of among my acquaintances

Your example 3:

_____
_____
_____
_____
_____
_____

What has the criticism to do with my life?

_____
_____
_____
_____
_____
_____

What would these same criticisms, leveled at me by others, have to do with their lives?

_____
_____
_____
_____
_____
_____
_____

Making fun of people and voicing gratuitous criticism is a group activity. It has the effect of temporarily forming a social bond among the members of the group based on a sense of superiority.

It's not worth it. The price you pay for indulging in this activity is anxiety about falling out of favor with that group and becoming subject to their scrutiny.

As with all the lessons, it is helpful for you to keep a record of your successes in achieving a goal. In this case, the goal is to put an end to your social and performance anxiety by opting out of the social rejection game.

A popular instruction for reducing the anxiety accompanying public speaking is to imagine the audience in their underwear. This is solid advice. If followed, it makes the speaker aware that the audience has its own "underwear" to attend to. And the speaker's "underwear" is none of their affair.

You can deal effectively with your social and performance anxiety by practicing a policy of limiting your attention to just what you are doing. If you are to speak publicly, what you say is your concern. If you are meeting new people, remembering their names and learning something about them is your business. Controlling their response to you is *not* your business.

Whether they practice superiority by social rejection is not your business. Participating in the social rejection game by making sure your underwear isn't showing will leave you with fear and trembling.

Practice Record For Lesson 9

Record your successes at leaving social rejection to others, minding your own business, and feeling calmer. Note that it is a trap to feel superior to others because they practice scornful gossip and you don't. You are just elevating the game to a higher level, the scorn of those who scorn. Minding your own business really means minding your own business.

Use your private notebook to record incidents in which you were able to relieve anxiety by reminding yourself to opt out of trying to avoid other people's social rejection.

These two examples will give you the idea:

Example 1: Date: 3/1

Incident: My husband and I were scheduled to go to a party that involved his business associates. These occur two or three times a year, and I hate them. I started worrying about it two weeks before the party. I know these people have relationships at work, and they gossip about each other's spouses.

Success: I asked myself what I wanted to accomplish at this party. I had to admit to myself that I wanted people to say good things about me and not laugh at me. I imagined myself as one of them and laughing at someone else.

It woke me up. None of us has any business doing that. I started to think of what my purpose at these parties really is. It is mainly to help my husband feel comfortable, try to remember names, find someone interesting to talk to, and have a good time. I felt relieved, as if I really had something to do there. I also felt a sense of being more mature and able to put the party into perspective. It's just one of those things we do. No big deal. I didn't even buy any new clothes.

Example 2: Date: 3/12

Incident: I'm chairman of the finance committee at our church. Every year I have to give a report in front of the whole congregation on the Sunday that we kick off our pledge drive. I hate it. This time I started to worry about it a month ahead, as usual. My palms started sweating just thinking about it.

Success: I started thinking about why I really do this. As much as I hate to admit it to myself, I connect being in an important position with feeling superior to others. As if they will look up to me and envy me. I considered what that kind of thinking costs me. I can't do it without feeling vulnerable to other people seeing that I'm a fake. Half of the people in the church probably are there for show. I decided that the only reason I do it is because it needs doing and I know how. I started thinking more about just preparing the numbers. My job that Sunday is to present numbers, nothing else. After thinking like this, the presentation seemed like just one of a dozen things I need to prepare for in the days ahead. It will only take a few hours, and then I can go on to something else until it's time to show up and give the report. I feel a lot more relaxed and energetic.

Lesson 10:
Misery as Anger

Consider how you feel around someone who is miserable. A parent who is unhappy, a spouse who is in pain, a child who is suffering, a friend who is going through a stormy time—any of these are likely to make you feel bad. Because misery can make others feel bad, it can be used as a weapon to punish and control them.

Just as vying for victim status (see lesson 5) so you can feel righteous when attacking others is a tool of anger, misery is a tool that can make others conform to what you want. Children learn to cry or appear physically ill in order to produce discomfort in their parents, to "make" the parents keep them home from school. Employees, as well as their employers, plead poverty to try to win concessions.

Nowhere is misery used as a weapon for control more than in families. Control struggles between parents and children are especially prone to its use. It is not uncommon for otherwise happy-go-lucky people to become fountainheads of misery when they become parents. It is as if they see it as their job description to worry, worry, and worry some more. What they don't see is that their worries about their children are meant to keep the children under control. These same parents, if they should happen to be working in supervisory positions, are apt to use misery as a supervisory technique at work. This gives them a double dose of everyday misery.

How does it work? It works because children care about their parents' welfare just as much as parents care about their children, at least to begin with.

- When your children "misbehave," your unhappiness is a potent punishment for the children. Your distress over something your children have done makes them feel bad and they alter their behavior. This rewards you for being distressed over their behavior.

- When your children change their behavior in order to keep you from being miserable, they reward your misery. Your misery becomes your tool for controlling them. This not only happens with parenting, it often happens with any sort of supervision.

- The more employees respond to your unhappiness with their performance, the more unhappy you become in order to get them to do what you want. Keep in mind that this is all about making someone feel bad as a tool to control them. Control of others is a difficult and tricky thing. But when you use your own misery to inflict hurt on others, you put yourself in a difficult position.

- The better your misery works for getting what you want, the more miserable you become. Indeed, that's the way it works. The more successful a tool is, the more it's used. Perhaps some of your misery really functions as anger.

Exercise 10-A: Discovering Misery that Is Anger

If you are a parent, supervisor, or both, think of three times in the recent past that you were unhappy in those roles. If you aren't either of these, think of three times that either a supervisor or parent was unhappy. Describe the incident, examine it to see if it made others unhappy, and then consider whether making others unhappy might have been the point.

These two examples will give you the idea and help you get started.

Example 1: My teenager had her nose pierced a few weeks ago. I didn't approve and told her so. I've been really unhappy about it ever since. Every time I look at her it makes me want to turn away.

Does the unhappiness make others unhappy? Well, I think she must be aware of how I feel. We've talked less lately, and she's been sort of artificially cheery when she talks to me. Now that I think about it, it's as if she's trying to cheer me up, and let me know that everything is OK. I guess she must be worried about how I feel.

Was making others unhappy the point of being unhappy? I certainly didn't like what she did. But I guess I have to ask myself why I'm still unhappy with her. "Unhappy with her"—that's interesting. That's the point, I guess. Showing my unhappiness is about her. It's sort of like I'm still punishing her so that she will not make me unhappy again.

Example 2: I work for a guy that must have ulcers. If he doesn't now, he sure will. He's always telling us how close the plant is to shutting down and how this order is absolutely critical or we will lose the customer with this worried look on his face.

Does the unhappiness make others unhappy? I should think so! This has gone on for a long time, but I still get a tight feeling in my gut when he goes into one of his "the sky is about to fall" routines. Everybody just sort of puts their heads down and turn into zombies when he does that.

Was making others unhappy the point of being unhappy? Now that I think about it, maybe that's how he thinks he needs to talk in order to make us serious about our work. I always thought he was just an unhappy guy. But maybe he thinks it's his job to be unhappy with us. If so, he's making a big sacrifice for the joint. He's obviously miserable all day long.

Your example 1:

_____

_____

_____

_____

_____

Does the unhappiness make others unhappy?

_____

_____

_____

_____

_____

Was making others unhappy the point of being unhappy?

_____

_____

_____

_____

_____

Your example 2:

_____
_____
_____
_____
_____

Does the unhappiness make others unhappy?

_____
_____
_____
_____
_____

Was making others unhappy the point of being unhappy?

_____
_____
_____
_____
_____

Your example 3:

_____
_____
_____
_____

Does the unhappiness make others unhappy?

_____
_____
_____

_____

_____

Was making others unhappy the point of being unhappy?

_____

_____

_____

_____

_____

Control of others through your misery is complicated by the fact that other people don't like you to control them, and they quickly "get it." They are apt to fight off your control with declarations of their own unhappiness with your behavior. Then the escalation of misery really begins. Competing for control by competing over who has the biggest cross to bear in life naturally leads to lots of self-pity.

Perhaps you have overheard people one-upping each other with recitations of their complaints. Perhaps you have entered into this competition with your child, your parent, your supervisor, or your supervisee.

It goes like this:

Kimberly's Mom:	"I'm always dead tired when I get home. And then I have to get your dinner and do your laundry."
Kimberly:	"At least you get to watch TV in the evening. I have to stay up until all hours doing my homework. I can hardly stay awake at school."
Kimberly's Mom:	"I know dear. School is the most important thing. That's why I work my fingers to the bone and go to work even when I have a migraine—so you can have the education that I never had."

> *Kimberly:* "I appreciate that, Mom. You're great. I just wish I had time to do something besides study and work at the restaurant. I don't even have time for my friends. I don't have the energy even if I had the time."

Exchanges like this between Kimberly and her mother leave both of them miserable. It is impossible to continually try to outdo others with proclamations of misery without keeping feelings of misery within reach at all times.

Added to Kimberly's constant self-reminders of how painful her life is, are her mother's displays of pain and suffering. This combination forms a depressing cloud over both of them. That the nature of this interaction between Kimberly and her mother is a control struggle is not yet apparent in the interchange.

Here's more:

> *Kimberly's Mom:* "You say I'm great, but you don't do much to help me around here."
>
> *Kimberly:* "What do you want from me? I have cramps, I've got homework to do, and my English teacher told me I'd better spend more time on my papers or I'd never get an A."
>
> *Kimberly's Mom:* "Oh, I'm sorry, Kimberly. I just feel so tired lately. I saw the doctor yesterday and she scheduled me for some tests. I didn't want to worry you, but you probably need to know what's going on."

Kimberly makes her play to control her mother's demands on her, only to be trumped by her mother's proclamation of the possibility of a serious medical problem. Not only has Kimberly lost this battle for control because her mother has established her right to feel more miserable than Kimberly does, but both of them now feel awful.

These two people, like many others, do not need to live their lives in misery. They both get along quite well, and are able, to a large extent, to choose where they put their energies.

Their misery is real, but manufactured to a large degree in order to struggle "effectively" with each other for control. They literally make themselves feel bad to make each other feel worse.

Exercise 10-B:
How to Stop Playing the Misery Game

The most generous gift you can give to your children, those who love you, and those you supervise, not to mention your friends, is for you to be happy. Then they are relieved of the responsibility to make you happy. Children and other supervisees are much easier to manage if they understand that your life is happy, and that what they do is of concern to you, but will neither spoil your life nor rescue your life's meaning and happiness.

Both you and your children need to understand that your future and your happiness is not dependent on whether or not they do things as you expect. It is their lives and happiness that is at stake, not yours.

In other words, make it clear that:
You do not barter your happiness for control over others.

Examine your feelings of unhappiness with your children or parents, your coworkers or boss, and your significant other. Try to locate areas of your unhappiness with them. "With them" are the key words to look for in your thoughts. Have you allowed your happiness to be dependent on their performance? How would you feel if you stopped trying to trade your happiness for a change in their behavior?

These two examples will help you get started:

Unhappiness with children or parents

Example 1: Our two-year-old boy is a mess. He screams and makes a scene whenever he doesn't get what he wants or we ask him to stop doing something. I get really angry with him and have even slapped him. I find myself being stern with him all the time. I feel really desperate and unhappy.

Is my unhappiness dependent on others' performance? It sure is right now. Sometimes my son is as nice as you please. I feel relief and enjoy him then. Other times he's terrible and I feel awful. When I get stern with him, he sometimes just laughs. I guess my life is under his control right now. That's not right.

How would I feel if I stopped trying to trade my unhappiness for a change in their performance?

I hadn't thought of it as a trade. Maybe I am trying to change his behavior by being unhappy with him. I remember in the beginning that I used to act unhappy with him when he did something bad. I didn't even feel the unhappiness then. I was just sort of putting on an act. When I think of giving up feeling unhappy with him, I feel like a fresh breeze comes over me. Maybe I could just treat his behavior like any other problem I have to solve: Get some advice and follow it. I can't leave my happiness in his control.

Unhappiness at work

Example 2: I'm a foreman at work. The people I supervise are a bunch of kindergartners. They squabble and complain all the time, and in the meantime the work goes undone. I have to work within union contract rules, so it's hard to come down on them. I'm really crabby with them, to put it nicely. Lately I've brought my irritation home and it's affecting my family.

How would I feel if I stopped trying to trade my unhappiness for a change in their performance?

How about if I just stopped being unhappy with them about their BS performance? Now that I think about it, the unhappier I am, the better they seem to like it. I can imagine just enforcing the rules that are in the contract, and letting the rest take care of itself. They wouldn't know how to respond to me if I was just matter-of-fact and hit them with a written warning. That's the way my general foreman is. I think they depend on my mood as a way to judge how thin the ice is. Wow, that would feel a lot better.

Unhappiness with children or parents

Your example 1:

_____

_____

_____

_____

_____

Is my unhappiness dependent on their performance?

_____

_____

_____

_____

_____

How would I feel if I stopped trying to trade my unhappiness for a change in their performance?

_____

_____

_____

_____

_____

Unhappiness at work

Your example 2:

_____

_____

_____

_____

_____

Is my unhappiness dependent on their performance?

_____

_____

_____

_____

_____

How would I feel if I stopped trying to trade my unhappiness for a change in their performance?

_____

_____

_____

_____

_____

Unhappiness with my significant other

Your example 3:

_____

_____

_____

_____

_____

Is my unhappiness dependent on their performance?

_____

_____

_____

_____

_____

How would I feel if I stopped trying to trade my unhappiness for a change in their performance?

_____

_____

_____

_____

_____

You have probably accumulated a good deal of misery in your life as a result of expressing your anger as misery. Your habit of trying to control family members by attempts to make them uncomfortable with your misery is likely to go way beyond your family. Remember that a good clue to use in tracking down the cause of misery is the use of the words, "I'm unhappy with them." You can also add "I'm unhappy with it" as a clue. The use of the word "with" rather than "that" or "about" is an indication that you are holding something or someone in the world responsible for fixing your unhappiness.

For example, would you ever say to your dying mother, "I'm unhappy with your dying?" If you did say such a thing, wouldn't it indicate that she was not supposed to die, or die differently, in order that you would not have to experience your unhappiness "with her"?

The interpersonal habit of making anger into misery tends to expand to the world in general.

If watching the evening news makes you miserable, then you are really into the misery control game. Ask yourself, "Am I unhappy with the law of gravity?" Well, that makes as much sense as attempting to bargain your misery with the world in order to change what's reported on the evening news.

There is plenty of misery in the world. Bad things have and will happen to you. You do what you can about them and tolerate the pains and sorrows that you cannot change. But there is no reason to continue to add to your misery by adopting it as a tool to carry around with you.

Recognizing your unnecessary misery and ridding yourself of it can be very rewarding. But at first you will need to practice separating the misery you have as a natural result of bad things that happen to you from the unnecessary misery that you carry around for no other reason than some hoped-for effect of demonstrating it.

This record form will help you set up your private notebook for keeping track of your successes in doing away with unneeded misery. The two examples show you how to record your success.

Practice Record For Lesson 10

Example 1: Date: 4/15

Area of unhappiness: Ever since our first child was born, my wife seems different. It seems as if we aren't that close anymore, and she is wrapped up in other things. I get angry with her sometimes, but I mostly feel lonely and depressed.

How my unhappiness was dependent on someone else's performance: When I thought about my unhappiness with my wife, I began to see that I had handed the control of what was to happen to my feelings over to her. My sadness was like a dead end. It just said, "I'm not going to be happy until you change." And there I sat waiting.

What I did: I got off my whining butt and said to myself, "This is ridiculous, I'm acting like the only thing I can do is be unhappy and wait for my wife to change and make me happier." A lot of the bad feelings about it just went away. At the same time I started being friendlier to her, and she has smiled more and taken more time with me.

Example 2: Date: 5/1

Area of unhappiness: My father has always been cold and unresponsive with me. I've spent a lot of my life feeling either angry with him or wishing he were different or would just let me know he loves me.

How my happiness was dependent on someone else's performance: My thoughts about being unhappy "with him" caught my attention and made me think maybe my unhappiness "with him" is really misery. Then it struck me like a lightening bolt, that for my whole life I've placed an important part of my happiness in his hands. I just put it there out of my control. I may as well have buried it.

What I did: When I go down that sad alley, I've started reminding myself that I'm putting myself in the position of a panting dog, waiting for a treat that he never gets. I feel a big weight lifted off my shoulders when I remind myself that I don't have to spend my efforts being miserable about what my father doesn't do. My life is mine. If what I do makes me miserable, that's in my control. But I'm not going to give that power to someone else.

Lesson 11:
Self-Control by
Self-Attack

The topic of anger directed toward yourself is part of the discussion of depression. Depression is a very large subject, and is mainly outside the content of this book. But if anger is habitually directed at other people so that you can exert control over them, it is also likely to be habitually directed at you for the purpose of self-control. It will be helpful for you to understand some of the consequences of self-attack, and to change how you approach doing or not doing things.

One problem with attempting control by attacking yourself is:
You respond no better to self-attack than you do to attack by others.

When others threaten you, you try to avoid the threat. A difficulty with attempting control by threats is that there may be ways to avoid the threat without doing what is wanted. When you threaten yourself, you try to avoid the threat in any way you can, not necessarily the way you intended. You are used to trying to find another way out when other people threaten you. You are likely to do the same thing with threats directed at yourself. A second problem with the use of threats for self-control is also usually present. When others threaten you, you become emotional and less able to solve problems rationally. When you threaten yourself, you also become emotional and stupid.

Most important, when others threaten you, you do not see them as friends and you struggle with them over control.

When you threaten yourself you experience a part of you as unwanted and unfriendly. You fracture your sense of self.

Most of us search for and value a calm mind. You will not find your way out of your stormy thoughts and feelings until you are able to govern yourself with a calm, steady, and gentle hand.

Exercise 11-A:
Discover Your Self-Control Technique

Here is a trick that will help you see what kind of self-control you practice. Think about three things that you want yourself to do or stop doing. Listen to what you think to yourself about each one. Then imagine another person saying these same things to you. People in therapy get the hang of this when they are asked to imagine a little elf always sitting on their shoulders, whispering the same things they tell themselves. Then evaluate whether the person (or elf) saying these things to you is a friend or an enemy. How would you react to someone else saying these things to you? These two examples will show you what to do.

Example 1: I want myself to pay my bills on time.

What I say to myself: "I need to do my bills. I've been putting them off like I always do. People will think I'm a deadbeat. My credit is going to go into the toilet. I've got to be a responsible adult."

Friend or enemy: Well, when I read these thoughts and imagine someone talking to me like that, it doesn't sound as if they like me very much.

How I would react to someone else saying these things to me: They sound condescending and critical and like someone is trying to shame me or scare me into doing something. My instinct is to react to that kind of thing by dismissing them and what they say. Or I might get angry and tell them they are full of it. Where do they get off implying that I'm not an adult?

Example 2: Make a dental appointment.

What I say to myself: "I just have to call. My teeth are going to fall out. I'll probably have dentures by the time I'm fifty. The dentist is going to be critical of me, or at least give me the cold treatment, if I wait too long."

Friend or enemy: Now that I read this it sounds like some of the things dentists and their tooth-perfect hygienists have said to me over the years. They operate on the principle that they are friendly to you when you are good, and like a critical parent when you've been bad. They aren't exactly enemies. It's just that their friendliness seems to be based on the condition of my teeth. Not a very comfortable feeling.

How I would react to someone else saying these things to me: I guess I'd react pretty much the way I react to the dentist when I'm at his office. I want out. The sooner I get away the better. Why can't they just treat me like a person and do their jobs and forget it? Hmmm. That was me talking about the way I talk to myself.

Your example 1:

_____

_____

What I say to myself:

_____

_____

_____

_____

Friend or enemy:

_____

_____

_____

_____

How I would react to someone else saying these things to me:

_____

_____

_____

_____

Your example 2:

_____

_____

What I say to myself:

_____

_____

_____

_____

Friend or enemy:

_____

_____

_____

_____

How I would react to someone else saying these things to me:

_____

_____

_____

_____

Your example 3:

_____

_____

What I say to myself:

_____

_____

_____

_____

Friend or enemy:

_____

_____

_____

_____

How I would react to someone else saying these things to me:

_____

_____

_____

Thoughts that lead to treating yourself as an enemy literally incorporate an enemy within you. You are one, made up of many parts, and like any other system made up of parts, if your parts don't get along, the health of the whole system suffers. Harmony within your mind is as important to your total health as harmony among your internal organs. Perhaps it is more important.

Can you imagine the effect on you if the cells of your heart muscle went on a work stoppage because the cells of your leg muscles took more than their fair share of oxygen while you were exercising? It isn't hard to imagine because that is a way of describing exercise-induced angina, the chest pain brought on by exertion in a heart patient. Clearly it is a sign of something gone wrong. Yet you go on work stoppages all the time when your inner voice takes an arrogant, unfriendly, and punitive approach to the rest of your mind. The pain you feel as a result may signal something worse for you than angina signals to a heart patient.

The bottom line is that threatening self-talk as a control attempt over your behavior breaks up the unity of your whole self and sets the stage for a stormy mind. Another is that it brings about emotionality. Lesson 2 shows the effects of increased emotionality on your intelligence and problem-solving ability—namely your IQ goes down.

Do you really want a stupid person paying your bills, or making out your income tax? Of course not.

Emotionality is a clue as to how to start ridding yourself of the quarrelsome and unfriendly part of you. In its place, you want to start to build a more effective and healthy way (literally) of managing your behavior.

Starting with lesson 2, you are being taught to substitute facts for judgmental thinking, to wait out anger before acting, to substitute friendly communication for anger in relationships, and a host of other approaches to your anger. Such teachings can be applied to management of your internal relationships among your decisions, behaviors, emotions, and intelligence. So, start with the first steps you learned to use in order to act intelligently.

- Tell yourself you are being emotional, and if you act or talk while you are emotional you will probably do or say something stupid.
- Tell yourself that when you are calm you can identify and solve the problem.
- Tell yourself to divert your thinking from "fuel-for-emotion" thoughts to something else until the emotion subsides.

These are the steps leading you out of anger to the rational behavior that you learned in lesson 2. They work to help you avoid the negative consequences of acting when you are angry. They can also help you avoid the negative consequences of attempting to govern yourself with emotion. The only change in these three steps is the substitution of "emotion" for "anger."

Unfriendly self-control comes down to pitting some form of fear against some form of dread. "I dread doing the dishes" is pitted against: "If I don't do dishes, people will think I'm a slob."

The idea is to avoid acting out of fear that is self-generated and to avoid fueling self-generated fear. This avoidance of fear deprives your unfriendly self from benefiting from its self-assumed throne of control. It also allows you to act intelligently. The key words are both "intelligently" and "act."

You don't avoid the problem that led to your attack on yourself, whether it is dirty dishes or making a dental appointment, by waiting out the emotion. You merely wait until you are calm to handle it. As with handling other kinds of anger, the idea is to apply your mind to the present problem, not on the emotion produced by the problem.

For example, the approach is:

- **The problem:** "I should make a dental appointment."
- **My emotional response:** "Yuck, I hate going to the dentist."
- **My attempt to pit fear against dread:** "I'll have to go or my teeth will get bad. He's already going to rag on me for not coming sooner."
- **My self-management intervention:** "Wait a minute—I don't want to make myself do something this way. I'm trying to scare myself. I'm treating my dread as the problem, rather than treating making the appointment as the problem. If I just calm down I can go back to feeling good."
- **My new approach:** "Well, what's the real problem here? Dental appointment. How do I do that? Look up the number. Hey, I'm not so sure I really like the dentist I've been going to. Sally told me about a new one in town that really treats her nicely. I think I'll call the new one."
- **The result:** I call the new dentist for an appointment.

You have a delicious surprise coming when you experience the ease with which you will be able to do things that you formerly put off and anguished over. You don't have to do things late and sloppily or drag yourself through them. Letting self-induced anguish and fear recede allows other, more subtle and tender feelings and emotions to appear. It is difficult to smell the roses while you are whipping yourself to cultivate the garden. A calm mind, like calm water, is more receptive and revealing of subtle and intricate patterns that affect it.

Exercise 11-B: Calm Self-Management

Start simply. Choose some ordinary tasks that you tend to avoid until and unless you threaten yourself with shame or fear in order to get yourself to do them. Ask yourself, "Do I want someone who is emotional and stupid doing this?" Resolve to stop fueling your fear and shame over the task until you can think of it calmly. Divert your thoughts and actions to something else until you can think calmly. Then consider what problem you are trying to solve.

Sometimes tasks look different when you are calmer and more intelligent and reflective. Try to catch yourself at a time when you are not thinking in terms of "having to do it," and say to yourself, "I think this is a good time to get that problem out of the way." Then concentrate on what to do first to solve the problem, instead of what to do to manipulate yourself.

Here are some examples before you try it.

Example 1: I need to do my income tax.

My emotional tug of war: I dread it. But I have to do it or I'll put it off until the last minute and I'll get fined for mistakes. I dread trying to find all the information I'll need. I've done a lousy job of keeping records. They put people in jail for making things up.

My intervention: Hold it! Calm down. I don't have to feel bad about this. Get out of here, feelings; you're not going to run this. I'm just sitting here. There is nothing going on to have bad feelings about.

The real problem: What do I need to get started? Get out the cancelled checks from last year. This is just a task. The whole thing is just to do something and then decide what to do next. I kind of like sorting through things and organizing them.

Example 2: I just have to clean the bathroom.

My emotional tug of war: I hate this. The place is filthy. I've let it go so long that I'm ashamed of it. We have guests coming over.

My intervention: These feelings are not pleasant and aren't solving anything. Calm down. I don't have to feel bad. I'm just sitting here at the kitchen table. The sun is shining and it is beautiful outside. There's nothing happening to make me feel bad.

The real problem: To clean the bathroom, what do I do first? Get out the cleaning supplies. That's simple. They smell kind of good in a funky way. I wonder what I could do to clean the shower without having to scrub so much? Well, I was going to exercise later, maybe I can do it by scrubbing.

Your example 1:

_____

My emotional tug of war:

_____

_____

_____

_____

My intervention:

_____

_____

_____

_____

The real problem:

_____

_____

_____

_____

Your example 2:

_____

My emotional tug of war:

_____

_____

_____

_____

My intervention:

_____

_____

_____

_____

The real problem:

_____

_____

_____

_____

Your example 3:

_____

My emotional tug of war:

_____

_____

_____

_____

My intervention:

_____

_____

_____

_____

The real problem:

_____

_____

_____

_____

It seems like a paradox, but it is the case that:
In order to manage yourself effectively, you must pay attention to the world outside of you, not the world inside of you.

You learn to pay too much attention to what's going on inside of you, rather than what's going on around you, when you grow up taking care of your feelings. You learn to manipulate your feelings by thinking certain thoughts, rather than by doing certain things. When a problem presents itself, you first try to solve the problem of manipulating your feelings and then expect that to result in a certain kind of behavior.

A healthier sequence when you are presented with a problem is to concern yourself with solving the problem and then taking the first step in solving it. This keeps you from turning every life problem into a manipulation of your feelings. The exclamation, "Just do it!" is mistaken as some sort of appeal to willpower. It is better understood as an instruction to "Take the shortcut around the struggle with your will and let the realities of the problem guide what you do."

Self-management can mean management of how you feel or it can mean management of your behaviors. Emotional responses need not be managed. They do need to be starved of fuel when they interfere with your life. If you feed your dread by making your dread the problem to solve before you can act, you have changed the task from getting something done to how you feel about it. It's like arguing with an obstructionist on a committee; you end up doing nothing while encouraging the obstructionist to do more obstructing.

In general, feelings are extremely important to us. But they are a bit like children; they can easily become unruly. If encouraged, the stronger and cruder feelings can easily become so boisterous that they not only drown out the others, they become the focus of your whole life.

Anger, fear, and dread are the names of some of the feelings likely to take over with their loud arguments. (Lust is in there too, but that's a story for a different set of situations.) Sometimes it is best not to try to out-shout them and instead, let them run down. Then you can get back to a calm atmosphere where your whole mind can contribute and be heard.

This lesson involves learning how to find a shortcut around dread, let it wilt, and get on with things you need and want to do. Once you start being able to do this it will be very rewarding. Practicing for a while and recording your successes in calm and friendly self-management will help launch you into a different way of approaching yourself.

Practice Record For Lesson 11

Follow these examples for keeping a record in your notebook.

Example 1: Date 6/5
Incident: I was putting off a project at work. I dreaded getting involved with it and as usual, I guess, I was waiting for the pressure

from my boss to get so high that I'd just have to do it or risk losing my job.

Success at friendly self-management: It occurred to me that I was just encouraging my dread and fear by delaying the project. One night about fifteen minutes before it was time to go home, I was feeling happy and calm, so I said to myself, "Why not get a start on that project? What will I need?" I spent a few minutes making a list of files that I'd need. Then I was sort of into it. I stayed late and finished the whole thing. It felt really good. For once I had time over the next few days to read and revise the project. I noticed along the way some things we could do to save money and included them too.

Example 2: Date: 6/10

Incident: My wife bought some bookcases for me to put up in my "hideaway room." They're the kind that has a million screws. I put off tackling them for weeks. I wanted to do it, but I dreaded it; and I guess I figured that after they had been there long enough, I'd feel like a lazy bum and get at it so I wouldn't feel any worse about leaving them sitting there.

Success at friendly self-management: One evening, I was trying to find a book, and it occurred to me that if those shelves were up, I wouldn't be hunting for things all the time. I just said to myself, "OK, what do I need to do to get started? Get them out of their cardboard boxes. Then get the tools I need." It occurred to me when I saw all those screws that my neighbor has an electric screwdriver. I borrowed it, and boy did that go fast. No big deal and it was kind of fun.

Lesson 12:
Learning To Use Your Will Without Anger

It is no accident that the term "willpower" includes the word "power." If you have an anger problem, you most likely try to will yourself or someone else to make changes. You put your will up against your "habit." Or you put your will against another person's will. Our language contains common phrases such as a "battle of wills" or "willful children," referring to those who don't roll over to be controlled by others. You probably don't roll over to "willful" control even of yourself.

When willing is made into an effort to control, it is merely an exercise in anger. When you put your will against something or someone, you have turned away from *behavior management* (carried out by your intelligence) over to *behavior control* (carried out by force). It's like a company that operates intelligently according to the facts most of the time, but sometimes, when its workers don't cooperate well, it turns to hired thugs. When you try to solve problems by putting your will against others, you are turning the solution over to an "enforcer," who, as the word suggests, uses force. An excellent place to begin the task of replacing willpower with an intelligent and competent will is in everyday hurrying through tasks.

This is because:
All hurry is anger.

What do you feel like when you are hurrying? Your shoulders hunch up. Your muscles tighten up. Maybe you wrinkle your forehead into an angry scowl. You actually feel as if you are trying to physically push against a barrier.

Compare these physical feelings to the way you feel when you are angry. In both cases, you are prepared to use force against something or someone.

If you have difficulty seeing your own hurry as an expression of anger, try observing others. People in a hurry on the street scowl and verbally attack others who get in their way. Drivers in a hurry stand on their horns when cars get in their way. Outright explosions of anger occur in families when people aren't ready to leave on time.

Try interrupting someone in a hurry. That is when they are most likely to be rude or worse. When people are hurrying, they are in attack mode. When hurrying, they are highly likely to become irritated, to swear and cuss, to say rude things, to attack their children and spouses, and to strike out. In other words, they are likely to do stupid things.

And doing stupid things is what angry people do.

So, hurry is where we start in order to change your angry will, which relies on power. Instead of an angry will, you want an intelligent will that relies on competence. You begin by slowing down when you are hurrying. You may say, "But suppose I need to or want to get something done quickly." To be quick is different than to hurry.

Doing something quickly requires skill and competence, not willpower and certainly not anger. Playing a fast passage on a musical instrument cannot be accomplished by just hurrying through it. It requires practice to achieve mastery. Practice doesn't consist of hurrying; rather, it usually consists of playing slowly with emphasis and good technique.

Similarly, doing your job faster requires increased mastery, not the will to hurry. Employers know as little about this as their employees, and consequently employers, set up powder kegs of anger in the workplace by increasing job output requirements without the opportunity for employees to master skills that will make them quicker at their jobs.

Accordingly, whether it's doing the dishes or getting ready for work, hurry is not what you want. Hurry is applying anger to your task. If you wish to be able to do something more quickly, you will need to increase your skill at doing it. Doing the dishes more quickly requires skill. Getting dressed and around in the morning more quickly requires skill. Moving more quickly requires skill. So remember:

- If you wish to speed up and you have a higher gear that you can comfortably shift into, do it.
- If you don't have a higher gear, don't hurry. Instead, look for a more efficient technique for doing the task. Then practice it.
- Shoot for a pace that gives you a sense of competence.

Exercise 12-A:
Recognizing Anger When You Hurry

You probably do a lot of hurrying, so it is easy to practice recognizing it and slowing yourself down to a pace at which you can perform competently. In the effort to do something about your anger, no other thing will bring you more peace than governing your "motor" to run at a comfortable pace.

You can practice this every day. To give you an idea of what to do, start by speeding yourself up while performing three simple tasks. Then observe how you are feeling, particularly the changes in your body tension. Then imagine allowing yourself to slow down again to a pace in which you can perform competently with smoothness and grace. Record what happens to your feelings and to your performance.

These two examples will give you the idea of how to perform.

Example 1: Doing dishes.
How it feels to hurry: I feel as if I'm physically leaning forward. I have the feeling of pushing myself. My actions get jerky and I have to pause frequently to kind of get back to what I'm going to do next. It feels tiring and unpleasant.

How it feels to "slow down": I relax and my concentration is on exactly what I'm doing. I can actually feel and pay attention to the way the water feels and hear the water running. I feel as if I'm actually doing something well. It's going faster than when I hurried, only it feels like a pleasant exercise of something I do well, like walking gracefully instead of like a klutz.

Example 2: Showering
How it feels to hurry: It feels as if I'm ahead of myself trying to pull my body and actions along. It feels as if I'm dragging something

heavy. I keep missing wet areas on my body while drying off with a towel. The whole thing feels like a big effort.

   How it feels to "slow down": I move more smoothly. I feel the water and it feels good. It's relaxing. I don't think I'm really taking any more time, but it feels as if I'm "here" while I'm doing it.

Your example 1:

_____

How it feels to hurry:

_____
_____
_____
_____

How it feels to "slow down":

_____
_____
_____
_____

Your example 2:

_____

How it feels to hurry:

_____
_____
_____
_____

How it feels to "slow down":

_____

_____

_____

_____

Your example 3:

_____

How it feels to hurry:

_____

_____

_____

_____

How it feels to "slow down":

_____

_____

_____

_____

When you are walking into a strong wind, you make your way by leaning into the wind. Using your will as a force to make something happen feels like leaning into the wind while walking. The difference is that your attempt to change yourself or another person with your will is what creates the wind blowing in your face.

You are preparing to attack when you put your will against someone. Part of that preparation is to become more tense. Muscle tension consists of each muscle contracting against an opposite muscle that holds the first muscle back (if that didn't happen, it would produce movement).

The sense of pushing against something, produced by willfulness, is a physical sensation produced by being held back with your muscle tension.

You may have experienced attempts to will a physical object to move. Bowlers, golfers, and others who observe an object moving sometimes use "body English." You lean your body in the direction that you want an object to move. Will used against an object isn't usually anger. The reason is that you actually move with your "willed direction." So it isn't experienced as pushing against something that holds you back.

But willfulness against yourself or another is anger. Making others comply with your wishes always involves some sense of trying to defeat their will; that is, substituting your control for theirs over their behavior. When you put your will against yourself, it will produce the same reaction in you that it produces in others, a sense of the impending danger of the loss of freedom.

Family relationships are where you are most likely to try to will others to do your bidding. Child management is particularly an area in which adults are vulnerable to the danger of pitting their wills against children. Some people even believe that children's wills need to be "broken." This amounts to the belief that growing up means to learn obedience in the place of individual freedom. It means that children need to learn to allow people in authority to decide their behavior for them.

Children as well as adults can be "broken" in this way. The result is the same as it is with an animal that has been broken. The result is a listless, depressed, spiritless, and—oh yes—obedient person. You must ask yourself if that is what you want to accomplish by putting your will against your loved ones, your spouse, and your children. If you are strong enough and mean enough and persistent enough, you might be able to actually substitute your will for theirs—if they aren't able to get away from you.

The result, if you think about it, would be truly depressing. You would be utterly alone, without the company of other living beings. Your companions would be the walking dead, robots that you produced for the sake of your wish to control them. You are fortunate that your family doesn't easily roll over to your will. They will resist and fight you, sometimes to the death. Parents have been known to spank their children so often and so long that the children go into shock and die. The great volume of blood that flows to the buttocks when they are repeatedly struck causes shock. Some children will take anything—including death—rather than submit. Does Patrick Henry, the man who demanded liberty or death come to mind?

For you, it is not likely you are at such an impasse. More likely you find yourself in perpetual battles with family members over whose will is to prevail. You push against them, clashing, without ever really resolving anything. Perhaps you can see that it's a good thing that you aren't able to prevail in your efforts to force your will upon them.

It will be an even better thing for you to stop trying to substitute your will for others'. Yes, you will say, "But isn't it a good thing if little Chucky behaves?" Or "Isn't it a good thing if Sally stops disrupting dinner?" Of course it is.

The problem is that if Chucky and Sally behave because they have allowed your will to be substituted for theirs, they will no longer be Chucky and Sally. They will be empty vessels.

If you stop and think about what you want, it is that you want your children to behave because they want to behave. You want your wife to reduce her extravagance because she wants to reduce her extravagance. You want your family to spend time together because they want to spend time together. These are all enviable goals. But they are impossible to accomplish by putting your will against your spouse or your children. To win that contest is to lose. They may do what you prefer, but because *you* want them to, not because *they* voluntarily want to.

Take a page from the history of governance. There has been a relentless historical march toward the substitution of the rule of law for the rule by a class, family, or one person's will. The rule of law breaks down when either there are so many laws that the decision of which laws to enforce is up to the will of a privileged class, or when the laws are not enforced, or when the laws function to make one set of people serve the interests of another set of people. Laws, when they are effective, make government predictable and are in the interests of the people governed.

Substituting rules—laws—for your will is the way to stop pitting your will against children or others under your supervision. The rules will only be effective if they benefit others, if there are only a few rules so that you need not choose which ones to enforce, and the rules make you predictable to those you supervise or parent. Be consistent.

Supervision without willfulness requires that you:

- Make sure the behavior you expect from others serves their interests.
- Make your expectations known.
- Be consistent.

Nothing is more destructive of good supervision than responses that escalate punishment for behaviors that don't meet the supervisor's expectations. For example:

1. Henry leaves his bed unmade.
2. Mom says, "Go make your bed. I'm only going to tell you once."
3. Henry continues watching TV.
4. Mom raises her voice, "Henry, I said go make your bed."
5. Henry looks at his mother with a pained expression and says, "Can't I do it when this program ends in five minutes?"
6. Mom says, "OK, but be sure and do it then."

7. The program ends and Henry starts watching the next one.
8. Mom screams, "You get to your room and make your bed now. No more TV for the rest of the evening."
9. Henry looks at his mother with hate and goes slowly toward his room.

Henry's mother has escalated her responses to Henry's non-compliance from telling him to make his bed (2), to telling him the same thing in a raised voice (4), to delaying her expectation (6), to screaming and punishing (8). Rule enforcement with escalating consequences always produces inconsistency.

Contrast the above escalating and angry style with:

1. Henry's mother says, "I expect you to make your bed."
2. Henry continues watching TV.
3. Henry's mother stands near him and says in the same matter-of-fact tone, "I expect you to make your bed."
4. Henry looks up at her and says, "Just a minute. I'll do it when this show is done."
5. Henry's mother continues to stand there. She says in the same tone, "I expect you to make your bed."
6. Henry says, "Oh, all right."

He gets up and makes his bed. Henry's mother does not get angry and goes about her business. Henry is more likely to make his bed the next day, but even if he doesn't, he will probably only have to be told once by his mother that she expects him to do it.

Exercise 12-B: Substituting Rules and Predictability for Willfulness

This is for parents, supervisors, teachers, or others who are in a position that gives them responsibility for the behavior of others. Choose three things you expect someone under your supervision to do. For each expectation record what you do now. Do you communicate your expectation? Is it in the interest of the person you supervise? Are you predictable when your expectation isn't met? Then make a plan as to how you will change your interactions with the person you supervise.

Two examples will give you a model for what to do.

Example 1: I expect my five-year-old, Johnny, to clean up his toys in the living room before going to bed.

What I do now: I tell him to pick up his toys when it's bedtime. He usually doesn't pay any attention. It becomes a real struggle with him. Sometimes I end up screaming at him. Sometimes I end up cleaning them up myself. Sometimes I end up sending him to bed without his evening snack, and he cries. I feel like it's not worth it.

Do I communicate my expectation? Yes, he hears it from me every night.

Is my expectation in the person's interest? I think so. I'm trying to teach him to keep things in order and to take care of his things. But it would be easier for me to just do the cleanup than to battle with him over it.

Am I predictable when my expectation isn't met? I guess not. When Johnny doesn't respond the first time, I raise my voice. Then when he doesn't respond, sometimes I yell, sometimes I threaten him with the loss of his snack, sometimes I start picking stuff up. I guess I'm all over the place.

Plan: OK, so the problem is being predictable. I need to decide on something I can always do and keep doing it when Johnny doesn't comply. Maybe I'll try just standing there and keep repeating, "Johnny, it's time to clean up your toys." It's going to be hard to keep saying the same thing in the same tone. I might have to stand there a long time. On the other hand, it's something I can always do and just thinking about it gives me a sense of relief. I won't always have to be thinking about how to make him pick up.

Example 2: I have this girl in my third-grade class who always turns in really sloppy and incomplete work. I know she can do much better.

What I do now: She isn't getting any better. I've tried everything, from writing notes telling her I think she can do better to talking to her parents. Of course, she's getting terrible grades.

Do I communicate my expectation? She knows she isn't doing what I want. But I guess it may not be clear to her what I expect on every assignment.

Is my expectation in the person's interest? Of course it is. It's her life that will suffer if she doesn't learn.

Am I predictable when my expectation isn't met? Well, I guess not. I've done all kinds of things. She does always receive a bad grade.

Plan: Well, the problem is to devise some way of letting her know what I expect in a better way and to always respond in the same way when she doesn't meet my expectation. Some of her work on assignments is acceptable. That could be an example to her of what I expect. Maybe instead of grading her papers right away, I could try to find something on each paper that is good, or something I can make a change in and easily turn it into what I want and expect from her. Then I will just hand it back to her and tell her to do it again. I could keep doing this and not grade the paper until it's all done well. That would make me predictable and would also let her know what I expect. She would also start earning good grades. I bet that would have a big influence on her.

Your example 1:

_____

_____

_____

What I do now:

_____

_____

_____

Do I communicate my expectation?

_____

_____

_____

Is my expectation in the person's interest?

_____

_____

_____

Am I predictable when my expectation isn't met?

_____

_____

_____

Plan:

_____

_____

_____

Your example 2:

_____

_____

_____

What I do now:

_____

_____

_____

Do I communicate my expectation?

_____

_____

_____

Is my expectation in the person's interest?

_____

_____

_____

Am I predictable when my expectation isn't met?

_____

_____

_____

Plan:

_____

_____

_____

Your example 3:

_____

_____

_____

What I do now:

_____

_____

_____

Do I communicate my expectation?

_____

_____

_____

Is my expectation in his/her interest?

_____

_____

_____

Am I predictable when my expectation isn't met?

_____

_____

_____

Plan:

_____

_____

_____

Whether you are responsible for another person's behavior or not, putting your will against theirs turns one problem into another. It turns the problem of getting what you want from them into the problem of winning a battle. Treating your own free will as if it is a source of power that forces you and others to do things will always lead you into battle against yourself and other people.

You have a center in your mind that can initiate action. But if you turn getting what you want into forcefully getting what you want, that center will always lead you into stormy waters. And the storm will be strongest at the center of yourself, your will to act, the source of your vitality.

A better model for your will—your volition—is a gentle and patient, but also persistent and intelligent, agent for action. You may find such a model by thinking back to a person in your life who believed in you. Perhaps there was a parent, a grandparent, or a teacher who regardless of your silliness and your failures, believed and had faith that your life would be good and that you would do well. If you combine reason and intelligence with that kind of faith in yourself, you will transform your stormy will into an effective source of vitality for your life. There is no problem in your life that can't be approached with intelligent problem-solving. Whether it is opening a package, doing the dishes, losing weight, resolving a conflict, or changing your behavior, you will be better off when you initiate intelligent problem-solving along with an expectation that the problem *will* be solved in that way, instead of pushing, attacking, and willing that it will be done.

Practice Record For Lesson 12

For a time it will be helpful for you to keep a record of your successes at substituting intelligent solutions for willful ones. These two examples will give you an idea of what to shoot for and how to set up your private notebook for recording your successes.

Example 1: Date: 10/9

Problem: I was having trouble making myself exercise. Sometimes I could make myself go to the gym, but it wouldn't last very long.

Success: I decided that I'd forget trying to push myself into going to the gym. Instead, I started thinking of ways for increasing my exercise every day. I came up with a whole list, including walking upstairs at work instead of using the elevator, parking in parking lots away from the entrance to stores, getting up from my desk at work at least every half-hour and attending to something that I needed to do elsewhere in the building. I stopped asking others to mail things for me and went to the mailroom myself. After a few days it began to feel so good to willingly walk that I started taking daily walks in the mornings.

Example 2: Date: 10/27

Problem: I hate football season. My husband watches every game on TV and it seems to go on forever. I keep trying to tell him enough is enough, and we fight.

Success: When I realized I was just battling wills with my husband, I started to think about what I could do to make things more pleasant for me. I called up some friends whose spouses also watched football. Several of them felt the same way I did. We decided to get together at each other's houses every Sunday during football season and play cards. The husbands can either take care of the children, or we can get baby-sitters. I think I'm going to look forward to football season now.

Lesson 13:
Voluntary Living

You cannot wade in the river of anger without being sucked in by the undertow of the loss of freedom. It is an outright logical impossibility to try to force yourself or someone else to do something and have the resulting behavior occur voluntarily. Participation in the exercise of force and threats of force can have only one of two results: either involuntary compliance or involuntary resistance. Neither can be made to seem free.

Unfortunately, you cannot always avoid people who threaten you in an attempt to control you. A mugger or a bully can only be dealt with by resistance, if possible, or by compliance if necessary. But most attempts by others to control you can be avoided if you don't feel you need or want something from the person attempting them. Other people most often employ threats that amount to withholding things they think you have some need of or claim to.

For example, coworkers who say something nasty to you can only draw you into the control game if those persons are unhappy with you and that is important to you. They aren't holding a gun to your head. They are merely holding their disapproval of you out as bait. It is only your "need" to control how they think of you that entangles you in a battle with them.

By now you have probably practiced enough of the lessons so that you can experience the possibility of peace that comes from stepping away from angry people and angry confrontations. You can change your life in a profound way by learning to cultivate the garden of voluntary living. A useful approach to cultivating voluntary living is to prune, wherever possible, transactions from your relationships with others.

Transactions are a necessary part of living with others. They are the agreements, formal and informal, that you make with others. They are promises, and so they are obligations.

Once made, they are mortgages on your future behavior until they are ended in some way. They consist of all the arrangements you make with others, from dinner engagements to bank loans. Attending school means you agree to do the work. Getting married means you agree to share your assets, remain monogamous, and share responsibility for children. Having children means you agree to care for them, even at those times when you don't feel your love for them. Every one of these arrangements is a transaction with its own set of obligations attached. And each of them, once made, represents some loss of voluntary living.

You choose many of these arrangements, and their resulting mortgages on your freedom, in order to enhance the overall quality of your life and add to your happiness. Problems arise, however, when you become too profligate in spending your future, making arrangements without thinking. The result is a life that is increasingly filled with obligations. This has two effects:

- Too many arrangements crowd out a sense of living voluntarily.
- Too many arrangements lead to problems of enforcing other people's compliance with the arrangements.

Together, the lack of a sense of living your life willingly and the constant attention to what you are owed, bring consequences that set the stage for anger. What to do? You will find that if you examine your life looking for the arrangements that you have accumulated with little or no thought, you will be able to drop many of them and regain a more balanced life, a life with important obligations, but with important freedoms as well.

Exercise 13-A: Finding "Obligation Bloat" in Relationships

Your closest relationships are likely to contain a large accumulation of transactions that were not there in the beginning and have contributed to increases in anger and decreases in pleasure. Think about your relationship with a significant other when you were starting out and first became an item. Much of what you did together felt voluntary. You spent time together and did things together willingly. You looked forward to being together.

Gradually the sense of spontaneity receded. Perhaps at first, if you decided together to go to the movies, it felt as if both of you wanted to go. After a while you began to feel that if you didn't go to the movies your partner would be hurt or angry. Perhaps at first, if you called your partner during the day, it felt as if you were doing so willingly and your partner enjoyed your call. Now if you don't call you feel your partner will be angry.

There are important and necessary arrangements that make relationships work. Keeping your word, being loyal, being trustworthy, and being dependable are the cornerstones of successful relationships. These are not voluntary once you have bonded with another person. But always calling during the day in exchange for your not being questioned when you get home, going to parties in exchange for keeping your partner happy, saying hello in a certain way in exchange for peace with your partner, always appearing interested in what your partner is saying in exchange for your partner's friendliness, and a host of other obligations are merely "bloat" that has accumulated over time. These behaviors bloat the relationship and rob both parties of the sustenance for voluntary interactions, actions done willingly.

Examine a close relationship and find three "arrangements" that have crept in that feel involuntary, and for which you have made no actual commitment. Make a plan for ridding yourself of each of these obligations. Making changes in these arrangements is likely to result in an attempt by your partner to enforce the "arrangements" with anger. This is only harmful if you make it into a battle. Just do what is within your power to do.

These two examples will help you get started:

Example 1: When we were first married, I didn't work and I enjoyed cooking meals. Now I work as much as my husband does and I still cook. I used to enjoy making him happy with a good meal. Now I just do it because he gets sullen if I don't. I guess the arrangement I have with him is that I cook and he doesn't get angry.

Plan: There's a big difference between making my husband happy and keeping him from being angry with me. One feels voluntary and the other feels like an obligation. There's a lot of that in our marriage. I need to talk with him about this. It's going to be hard not to fight with him about it. If we can't get anywhere, maybe a marriage counselor would help. In the meantime, I think I'll stop making it my job to keep my husband from being angry by cooking every night. I'll tell him we both need to take care of cooking. Maybe we can agree to my cooking if he cleans up afterward. If he doesn't agree on some change, then I'll start fixing meals for myself when I feel like it.

Example 2: When we first began to go together, I started social-izing with several of my wife's friends. Now I feel obligated to par-ticipate with her in all of her arrangements with them. I've pretty much lost contact with old friends of mine. I guess socializing with her friends and not mine became part of our marriage contract.

Plan: I never agreed to this arrangement. I just went along with it. I think I'll suggest inviting some of my friends over or going out with them instead of always going out with her friends. She doesn't have to participate if she doesn't feel like it. I can plan more outings than I have been doing. I hope she will come along sometimes, but we don't always have to do the same things.

Your example 1:

_____

_____

_____

Plan:

_____

_____

_____

Your example 2:

_____

_____

_____

Plan:

_____

_____

_____

Your example 3:

_____

_____

_____

Plan:

_____

_____

_____

A common path people take is to keep filling up their lives up with transactions because they feel overwhelmed by the transactions they have entered into already. This paradox occurs because the act of entering into a new agreement feels like a breath of freedom. For example, you feel depressed and lifeless because every day seems like nothing more than doing what you have to do. So you go shopping for a toy, a new car, a four-wheeler, or just some new clothes. Chances are you will use a credit card. The shopping felt good and was voluntary. The purchase felt good and was voluntary. Paying for what you bought is not voluntary and merely adds to the burden of obligations you have already accumulated.

This pattern is common. It often leads to a point where all obligations are thrown away in the interest of finding relief. The marriage, support of children, payment of debts, and work obligations are all thrown away in one grand attempt to "get a life." This revolt is often triggered by anger, fueled with self-righteousness born of the feeling that one is not appreciated. In other words, others don't keep their side of the assumed arrangements you have been living with. You think that the things you accumulate are supposed to make you happy in exchange for what you have paid for them. They don't. You think that your wife is supposed to make you happy in exchange for marrying her. She doesn't. You think that you are supposed to be appreciated at work in exchange for making yourself do your work. Your boss doesn't. Wherever you feel obligated, you assume there is something owed you in return. It isn't.

You aren't owed anything except those things you actually contract for with another person. Most of what you feel you have coming is not owed to you at all. The feeling that you are owed something and aren't getting it leads to anger. The problem is that there never was a contract for most of what you feel obligated to do.

Voluntary living consists of intentionally limiting your transactions to the minimum necessary for your well-being and happiness. This leaves the rest of your life free. Your relationships are then dominated by give and take. And the "give" part is a real gift, not an obligation. Your activities are dominated by those things you love to do. And the "love" part draws you toward what you do, rather than having to drive yourself toward what you do.

Exercise 13-B:
Taking Charge of Your Life

Examine the way you live, looking for those things you have to drag yourself kicking and screaming to do. Ask yourself what transaction set up those behaviors as obligations. If there is a transaction in effect, are you receiving what you contracted for? If not, why are you obligated? Can you improve your life without this obligation?

Find three obligations that don't make any sense and that you are willing to eliminate.

These two examples will help get you started:

Example 1: I feel that I must keep the house spotless. My mother always did, and I feel guilty if I don't.

What was the transaction? I guess there really wasn't a transaction. It's more as if I feel that if I don't do it, I'm letting my mother down.

Are you receiving what you contracted for? I'm not receiving anything. My mother isn't here to give me her approval. All I'm getting is tired of cleaning.

Are you really obligated? Absolutely not! It's just the feeling that I have that I must do it.

Can you improve your life without this obligation? Well, maybe I could get used to just cleaning on a regular schedule like other people do. It would leave more time to do something I want to do. Maybe I could enjoy myself watching TV with my husband in the evening instead of irritating him by running the vacuum. I've always wanted to take up quilting.

Example 2: We have these friends who always invite us to do things. We always seem to say yes because we feel we can't hurt their feelings. Then we have to invite them to do things and it goes on and on.

What was the transaction? I guess there isn't any, except the idea that accepting their friendship is something we ought to do. They are nice people. They're just not much fun to be around.

Are you receiving what you contracted for? I don't see what we really agreed to. They don't owe us anything.

Are you really obligated? I guess we aren't. They will probably glom on to some other couple if we stop seeing them.

Can you improve your life without this obligation? It would feel like freedom. We might actually enjoy seeing them once in a while if we stopped doing it out of obligation.

Your example 1:

_____

_____

What was the transaction?

_____

_____

_____

Are you receiving what you contracted for?

_____

_____

_____

Are you really obligated?

_____

_____

_____

Can you improve your life without this obligation?

_____

_____

_____

Your example 2:

_____

_____

What was the transaction?

_____

_____

_____

Are you receiving what you contracted for?

_____

_____

Are you really obligated?

_____

_____

_____

Can you improve your life without this obligation?

_____

_____

_____

Your example 3:

_____

_____

What was the transaction?

_____

_____

_____

Are you receiving what you contracted for?

_____

_____

_____

Are you really obligated?

_____

_____

_____

Can you improve your life without this obligation?

_____

_____

_____

Obligations come from contracts. That is why they are a source of anger. When something is owed to you and not paid, you have the right to meddle in the affairs of the person who owed you. For many people this means attacking the "delinquent" with righteous indignation.

And, of course, people are apt to claim they don't owe anything, or they paid already, and then they, in turn, become righteously indignant.

You can avoid much of this quagmire by simplifying your obligations, paring them down to those that are desirable, and by avoiding taking on additional obligations without thinking them through. This part of your life, the transactional part, is necessary in some measure. But the spice of your life, the part that gives you vitality and energy for living, is your free interaction with people and problems. Keeping as much of your life free for interacting without obligation and without expectation of specific payment from others will make your life feel voluntary and make it voluntary.

Practice Record For Lesson 13

It is necessary to practice voluntary living in order to achieve it. Keeping track of successful changes that you make will help you get started. These examples will show you how to set up your private notebook for recording your successes.

Example 1: Date: 11/5

Success at balancing obligation and freedom: My wife and I sat down and did an inventory of our financial obligations. We've both been working as much overtime as we can in order to keep up with what we still owe. I decided I can do without the snowmobile and she decided she could do without her racy little convertible, especially if it meant not having to work overtime. We got out from under both debts and reduced our monthly payments by over five hundred dollars. We figure we have to actually earn seven hundred to bring home enough to make these payments, so we saved way over what we earned working overtime. We both feel good about this and are talking more now that we have more time. We are also planning other changes in the way we live.

Example 2: Date: 11/20

Success at balancing obligation and freedom: I was in a relationship that I didn't like and wasn't enjoying. I asked myself why I felt I should keep it up. I realized that I felt obligated to this guy to keep him from becoming unhappy. I don't know how I got into such a state. Maybe it was in order to feel good about myself and feel as if I was the only one on whom he could depend. When I thought about it in those terms, it became obvious to me that I had made a bad deal. It really wasn't hard to correct once I was willing to give up feeling as if I was his savior. That wasn't much of a payment for all the time and energy I used up seeing him. Now I feel much freer, and even better, I feel as if I can examine other parts of my life and do something about them.

Concluding Note

The rewards that await you as you examine the role anger plays in your life are difficult to overstate. Each lesson in this book has its own story and will connect with your life in a different way. You will benefit by reviewing some of the lessons repeatedly. Change is hard, but the results that await your efforts are more than worth it. You can achieve a calm mind, more satisfying relationships, more subtle and discriminating feelings, a more refined capacity for problem-solving, and a sense of living your life voluntarily. These rewards are worth the journey.

About the Author

Carl Semmelroth, PhD, has maintained a mental health practice for over twenty-five years in Kalamazoo and Coldwater, Michigan. He received his doctorate in psychology from the University of Michigan.